WHAT THE PRUDENT INVESTOR SHOULD KNOW ABOUT SWITZERLAND

and Other Foreign Money Havens

Bear Markets—How to Survive and Make Money in Them

A Treasury of Wall Street Wisdom

The International Monetary Muddle

HARRY SCHULTZ

What the Prudent Investor Should Know About Switzerland

and Other Foreign Money Havens

ARLINGTON HOUSE   New Rochelle, New York

Ninth Printing, January 1974

Library of Congress Catalog Card Number 76-130297

ISBN 0-87000-105-1

MANUFACTURED IN THE UNITED STATES OF AMERICA

To Dawn Schultz, my favorite economist.
She was both sunrise and sunset for this book.
Her research and ideas were indispensable.

Acknowledgments

Thanks to Michael Schemmann of Switzerland for his information on Swiss Banks.

Thanks to Dr. Werner Meyer, former economic editor of National Zeitung of Switzerland, for reviewing the manuscript for authenticity.

Thanks (for economic inspiration) to Professor W. von Hayek, Dr. Hans Sennholz, Antony Fisher, and Henry Hazlitt.

Perhaps we should add the names of John Maynard Keynes and Karl Marx and their like, who made this book *necessary.*

Contents

"It is a socialist idea that making profits is a vice; I consider the real vice is making losses."   Winston Churchill

Why should one invest abroad? . . . the principle of eroding values . . . explores the principle that in times of boom, one invests in stocks and bonds and real estate, etc., without giving a thought to the fact that *money values* (or buy-power) are not constant, that inflations (etc.) can erode a large measure of capital or profits or both . . . that in times of depression and recession, even if you sell short and buy contra-cyclical shares you are not hedging against deflation and devaluation which can counteract much of any profit you may have made . . . America—strongest country in world? . . . loss of value . . . explains why, at certain times in the business cycle, even free and otherwise sensible countries erode by legislation the REAL value of currency which eats away the value of your investment . . . how buying long or selling short and investing on a purely *national* basis are only profitable in times when the value of the currency in which the investments are denominated remains stable . . . the need to think independently . . . how at times, when monetary instability and political unrest set in, it becomes necessary to take Thomas Jefferson's advice and realize that "A merchant (i.e. businessman or investor) has no country" and seek stability and *constant values* elsewhere . . . how inflation, deflation, stop-go mechanisms, controls and other political maneuvering can kill the true VALUE of your assets regardless of how you invest, if you only think nationally.

Why man trades . . . a standard of value . . . how money first came into being as the compromise between man's desire for total freedom and his desire to make the best use of the world in which he found himself by specializing and trading . . . how much freedom need be lost by trade . . . how freedom can only be preserved via a sound currency, enabling man to trade his talents and abilities where he chooses . . . causes of inflation . . . inflation and taxation . . . historical forms of money . . . a store of value . . . slavery and money . . . when to act alone . . . on prognosticators . . . on politicians . . . the approaches governments use to delude the public into believing that nothing that is not "good for them" has happened to their currency . . . the need to act BEFORE the wrongs are obvious.

Brief outlines of what happened in various periods of currency erosion in Rome at the fall of the empire . . . France in the 1790's . . . Germany during the post-WWI era, the pre-WWII era, and up to end of WWII, and how the German "economic miracle" was largely a matter of correct government policy . . . the economic decline and fall of the British Empire . . . the USA during the Civil War and the various depressions and currency upheavals before and since . . . a quick look at South America and the Middle East where EVERYBODY who is anybody has his money permanently locked in a Swiss bank . . . an analysis as to what action one should have taken in these various crises by investing abroad and at what point one should have moved assets . . . what happened to those who didn't and tried to preserve them at home (e.g. bankruptcy and prison and even death) . . . how much inflation can we live with? . . . a sum-up as to how governments, well meaning though they might be, have consistently bankrupted their citizens, historically, and done the wrong thing—when knowing everything was going quite wrong, have sworn things never looked better, and how after a very few years have left their countries and people in social ruin in a way that even wars never do.

Modern history . . . the state of world currencies today . . . what erosion has taken place . . . how much value has been lost as a result . . . what measures if any have been taken to counteract this . . . gold . . . what measures have been taken that have made things even worse . . . the problems of Great Britain today . . . basic economic forces . . . government methods . . . inflation and velocity . . . the US gold hoard . . . how buying power has diminished over the years . . . what is the inflation rate?

Part 2: Foreign Havens (the "Where" Factor)

If one cannot always invest nationally (with prudence) then where? . . . reasons for looking abroad . . . what one looks for in a money haven . . . what it must have that one cannot find in one's own country . . . *needs* a stable currency . . . a history of neutrality in the foreign country . . . banking privacy . . . lack of government intervention . . . a democratic country, with political stability . . . conservative banking laws . . . a sound backing for the currency . . . internationally recognized status as a money center . . . reciprocal laws between the country in question and your own . . . freedom of movement of currency in and out the country . . . stability as a national characteristic . . . how to check out a foreign country.

Methods for investment abroad . . . a discussion of the various places where it is relatively easy to invest abroad, e.g. Japan, Germany, South Africa, Canada, Australia, etc. with the merits of each weighed . . . discussions from the point of view of actual investments in these places plus the merits of the currency involved in relation to exchange control, how closely tied to dollar or pound and why this matters . . . what sort of stocks and shares they have to offer and what would happen to them should the United States of America and GB "go under," fiscally, leading to the main conclusion that the easiest way to invest in most other countries is through a Swiss bank because there are not only banking institutions but international brokerage houses.

A discussion of how to buy gold, silver, diamonds . . . shorting and buying other currencies, the principle involved, how to do it . . . making loans in other countries and Eurodollars . . . trust agreements . . . time deposits . . . other international paper . . . again pointing out that all can be done through a Swiss bank . . . gold markets . . . kinds of funds sold abroad.

Part 3: Swiss Banks (the "Who" Factor)

The facilities a Swiss bank can offer . . . a discussion of the types of accounts that one can open . . . the trading department of a Swiss bank . . . how do you buy stocks, bonds, commodities, etc. through a Swiss bank . . . the cost of doing this . . . explanation of banking departments, investment departments, trading departments . . . how they handle margin . . . buying silver through a Swiss bank . . . what they do and do not charge you for . . . numbered accounts . . . regular name accounts . . . the joint account . . . holding items in "safe deposit" in a Swiss bank . . . underwriting . . . wills . . . Swiss companies.

A fair appraisal of the rumors that circulate about Swiss banks . . . Swiss bankers do not bring down currencies . . . hideouts for gangsters? . . . deposed and exiled monarchs . . . numbered accounts; are they really necessary? . . . tax evasion . . . "the gnomes of Zurich" . . . do they actually pull the strings of world money and overthrow governments? . . . do they truly have more knowhow? . . . Swiss interest in money . . . what Swiss banks really are . . . Swiss secrecy . . . what sort of people are their customers . . . how much or how little pressure can be exerted by foreign governments . . . Switzerland and taxes . . . what Swiss banks are *not* . . . how they got their aura of mystery . . . Swiss neutrality for 600 years, stable currency, world bankers, etc.

The Swiss as a people . . . how there is *no* such thing as a *Swiss,* only Zurichers, Bernese, etc., and so WHERE you decide to live *in* Switzerland is all-important . . . discussion on "how it would be" culturally, living in the various parts of Switzerland . . . discussion on how your taxes are affected if you become a resident of Switzerland, as a) working b) retired-not working . . . outline of Swiss tax system . . . requirements for residency and how to go about getting it . . . day-to-day problems of living in Switzerland (TV, newspapers, etc).

Part 4: Method (the "How" Factor)

The mechanics of opening an account *abroad* in ANY bank in any country, and Switzerland in particular . . . foreign affiliates of US banks . . . foreign brokerage houses . . . foreign branches of US brokerage houses and what they do . . . communications (i.e. whom do you write to and who writes back and how) . . . how often you get statements if at all . . . power of attorney pros and cons . . . how you will know what they have done for you . . . can you visit your money? . . . how the customer-banker relationship is different . . . a list of foreign banks . . . Swiss banks abroad . . . do you have to know a foreign language to bank and invest abroad?

The headaches of investing abroad . . . problems of language, and even if they write in English it is not American-English and the problems which result . . . problems of getting quotes on the foreign stocks, etc., one buys . . . problems of receiving bank statements that look quite different from anything you have ever seen before . . . problems of different accounting systems and because foreign banks *do* more, errors can be worse, necessity to check all statements, etc, thoroughly . . . *how* to check . . . *how* to complain to get best results . . . international investment letters.

Not intended to be tax advice as given by an accountant or tax lawyer, but as a guide on various taxes one may be liable for if one makes money abroad in various ways . . . interest equalization taxes . . . how (only) Americans are taxed on worldwide income, etc. . . . Americans living in the USA with foreign income . . . how the onus to declare is on the individual . . . Swiss taxes imposed "at source" . . . the reciprocal tax laws with foreign countries where they take the taxes off the top and you must then declare to US government to get a rebate . . . how if you also RESIDE abroad you still pay US tax, though less . . . tax havens . . . how advisable to consult tax lawyer if you intend to invest large amounts abroad . . . could get complicated.

Contains a glossary of foreign banking terms which you may find on your bank statements and confirmation slips . . . because foreigners think differently they value different things and the American has to quell a sense of frustration when he receives seemingly hostile letters, slow service, etc. . . . that Swiss lack of "flair" is a good not a bad thing . . . but has to be lived with and can be difficult . . . pictures of foreign bank statements and explanations . . . also a few words on the mentality of various foreign bankers.

Part 5: Timing and Outlook (the "When" Factor)

How you will know when to bring your money home . . . the signs you will see . . . the things that must have happened by that stage . . . the mechanics of selling and coming home . . . closing your account abroad . . . the time lag in getting rid of certain foreign types of investment, etc. . . . the advantages of keeping some part of assets abroad permanently.

How predicting the sequence of events is easier than timing . . . an attempt to put a time scale on the erosion talked about . . . where we are now . . . the sequence in which it could happen in the future . . . what to buy when it IS all over . . . some basic investment philosophy.

US laws on foreign accounts . . . legislation always threatened . . . letters to Switzerland—mail, to and fro . . . Swiss banks abroad . . . listing of major US and foreign banks in key European cities . . . summary of Switzerland by Colonel Harwood from political-economic-historical view . . . typical tax haven—Curacao . . . sources for further information.

SETTING THE THEME——

"A merchant has no country."

THOMAS JEFFERSON

Sauve Qui Peut

(approximate English translation)
"Whoever can do so, save himself."

"The most important thing about money is to maintain its stability, so that a dollar will buy as much a year hence, or ten years hence, or fifty years hence as today, and no less. With paper money this stability has to be maintained by the Government. With a gold currency it tends to maintain itself even when the natural supply of gold is increased by the discovery of new deposits, because of the curious fact that the demand for gold in the world is practically infinite. You have to choose (as a voter) between trusting to the natural stability of gold, and the natural stability, and honesty and intelligence of the members of the Government. And, with due respect to those gentlemen, I advise you, as long as the Capitalist system lasts, to vote for gold." . . . GEORGE BERNARD SHAW

All the currencies shown were issued by their governments in good faith, but have since become totally worthless. Except one. The one in the middle. Only the Swiss Franc has retained its hardness over the years, and it's largely because the Swiss currency is so hard that Switzerland is a safe harbor for your money.

PART 1

*Principles of Eroding Value
(the "Why" Factor)*

CHAPTER 1

Introduction

"A little inflation is like a little pregnancy—it keeps on growing." Leon Henderson

"The first panacea for a mismanaged nation is the inflation of the currency; the second is war. Both bring a temporary prosperity; both bring permanent ruin. But both are the refuge of political and economic opportunists." Ernest Hemingway.

MOST books on investment have been written as guides to investing within *one* country. They also start with the premise that capital appreciation is the art of increasing the *numerical* count of the currency in which the investment is denominated.

The aim of *this* book is first to break away from the one-country concept, and second to show that the way to safeguard one's assets and hopefully increase one's capital is to increase the *value* of one's holdings, not just the numbers of bills in which the value is denominated.

To illustrate the latter: a man who bought a house in England in 1935 for £1000 may now be able to raise £3000 on it. However in actual terms of buying power he has *not made a dime* (or a shilling) because the pound has lost two-thirds of its value during that period of time.

The Principle of Eroding Values

Value is a much underrated commodity. These days we are so used to dealing with credit, paper money, etc. that we never stop to think that value is basically the worth of one item that can be traded for another item which can be traded. The monetary paper we get in exchange for our first trade is really an IOU defined in terms of our other needs. For example, if when we made our first trade we knew that the money we raised by selling our automobile would buy three expensive Swiss watches, we would be very unhappy when, a year later, we discovered that we could only buy two watches with that money. Yet that is exactly what happens when government actions, war, disasters, etc. change the value of currency. It is largely to offset this that this book has been written.

We know of no way to *fully* offset this factor on a *national* basis. When a currency in any country begins its downward journey in value, then the pattern is always the same: the increase of controls, and the loss of value of one's assets—which does not fully show until deterioration is severe. Then somebody in government belatedly recognizes the downtrend and is forced by chaos and hardship (caused by sliding values) to devalue (i.e. revalue the currency in terms of gold). The best way to counteract this is literally to move out of *accepted* capital investments and go elsewhere. If you go back and read through biographies of the big money names, such as Bernard Baruch, or such famed market analysts as Robert Rhea, it will amaze you how many said in 1929, *not* "let's short" or "let's get completely invested in *things* instead of shares or cash," *but rather* they said: "this is the time to take a holiday from the stock market and I'm taking one." Generally they meant a holiday abroad!

But why abroad? To find a constant store of value when your own currency is *not* constant. If a market goes down, or inflation sets in, then cannot one just go short and counteract this by internal speculation? Perhaps the answer to this can best be explained if we glance back at the last big money-eroding period in the United States of America . . . that of post-1929. This will be a deflationary

Some of the leading
Stock Markets of the World

London

example but we could as easily produce an inflationary one. They are equally deadly. In fact we'll deal with inflation properly a bit later.

In 1929, if you had been one of the big plungers, and had an intensely strong nervous system, AND also had been absolutely right in your timing (though nobody ever is), you would have shorted near the top with your *liquid* capital and covered near the bottom (but nobody ever does that either). You would then have taken that cash and bought blue chips, and if you had been a super genius you would have been one of the few who foresaw 1937, before it fell, out of a blue sky, and sold at the top there too. You would obviously have made far more money than virtually anybody else who lived through that fiasco.

However, the value of your house and land and office building and art and miscellaneous valuables in that same period would have dropped more or less as badly as stock market values. So what you made on your stocks would have been lost on the falling value of your other assets. Then, when Roosevelt devalued the dollar by approximately 40%, the REAL value of your investments would have further diminished. Let me illustrate with some specifics.

Let's assume the total value of your assets in 1929 was a quarter of a million dollars. That $50,000 was tied up in your house, another $50,000 was in your office building and business, and that there was $50,000 in miscellaneous assets (including your cars, wife's jewelry, and antiques). And you had $100,000 cash to invest.

Let's imagine that you were amazingly clever and that near the end of 1929 when the Dow was at 300 you said "This is it" and went short with that $100,000. Let us assume you were satisfied with a market fall of 67% and so you covered at about DJIA 100. This means for every

300 dollars you invested you made 200 dollars and therefore your $100,000 had increased to about $170,000. Not bad. Now what about the other assets you have? Most values dropped far *more* than 50% in the depression, and worse than that, there were few or no buyers at any price for most things. However, let's assume that the rest of your assets merely dropped 50%. Your non-cash assets of $150,000 would now be worth $75,000. This gives you (a market genius) an asset value in 1932 of $245,000 as opposed to the $250,000 you started with in 1929. Well you did better than your friends I am sure. However, then Roosevelt devalued the dollar by approximately 40% in 1934 which promptly put your assets at a little under $150,000, a total loss in VALUE of $100,000. On the other hand, if in 1929 you had sold all your assets, maybe just keeping the business overhead at minimum (selling the building and renting), sold your house (and later bought another at the bottom), put your liquid assets into a currency that looked sounder than the dollar (to escape devaluation), then not only would you have been able to sleep nights (being short 40% of one's assets is nerve-racking) but you would have fared a *lot better.*

America—Strongest Country in the World?

"Ah," you say. "But things are different now. America wasn't as strong then as she is now. Today she is a superpower and surely is the land of greatest opportunity in the world?" But do you realize that it is a contradiction in terms? America WAS indeed founded on freedom, and responsible freedom gives greatest opportunity. America reached its peak of freedom and capitalism about 1910. It became a world power with World War I and unfortunately became a superpower with World War II. But power means power *over* somebody, so freedom and power CANNOT go together. The very nature of a super-power is her greatest weakness. As a superpower she has to drain her resources to protect, supply arms to, attempt to feed, and generally police half the world, with Russia trying frantically to make that half smaller. As a super-power a government needs to be legally strong, in order to marshal resources. Taxation powers and appetite grow. Government grows. Freedom diminishes. A government that has the power necessary to give everything also has the power to take everything away.

Loss of Value

Today in America costs are rising rapidly, which is merely the currency losing its VALUE. As illustrated in the story earlier about the automobile and the Swiss watches, the same applies to your cost of living. If your wages buy *less* now than they did a year ago, unless there has been a natural disaster to make foodstuffs short (or unless you are working fewer hours, thus earning less), it isn't because the relationship between your job output and your requirement of essential commodities has changed, but that you find the same amount of currency buys less. . . . which is loss in the *value* of the currency.

The Need to Think Independently

Californian economist John Kamin made this statement in June 1969: "One by one all avenues of escape are being closed to the average investor. Whipsawed in the stock market, wiped out in commodity markets, with bank credit cut off and time purchases curtailed, he is being forced into an ever tighter straitjacket. All doors are slammed shut and locked behind him. *Unless* he is a truly independent thinker and an investor who views probabilities in an international manner, a highly flexible person who moves capital freely from country to country, there isn't much hope for him."

This of itself points to the arrival of a period of history when to invest for *numerical* appreciation is no longer prudent. The prime time for investing on that basis is of course in times of *constant* valued currency. But today, devaluations are commonplace, and even the mighty dollar, which as of this date has not yet been devalued, is showing its internal loss in value via rising costs.

When this happens, then the time has come to look for other havens for money placement, to "take that holiday," and find a currency and country where values, at least for the moment, are more or less constant, or at any rate more constant than those at home.

Twentieth Century Economics

Whether or not America is politically going quite wrong is outside the realm of this book. Political aspects are necessarily tied in with the economic, but we shall concern ourselves here only with the political ramifications of economic policies—not politics itself. In 1929 things were going badly, and yet those in power seemed powerless to do anything *right* to stop them. They started out by denying most of the way down that anything *was* wrong. Then Roosevelt came into office. He admitted things were wrong, and took upon himself all sorts of unprecedented authority to put matters right, and he did alleviate the situation for the near term. But at high cost to the future. Longer term his plans for a "New Deal" were so disastrous that the depression lasted more or less until the false economic impetus of World War II boosted the American economy back into life (i.e. 1932–1942) and when the war was over the problems were back. They were "solved" only by buying time, a la Keynes, not by creating foundations to last over the next century or so.

The history of the 20th century will surely be written as one when man reached new heights of technological progress and new depths of monetary muddle, debt, and chaos. World War I caused inflation which helped cause a depression which caused governments to inflate, which caused hardship, all of which in some ways can be said to have fomented World War II. That war in turn caused more inflation which brought about devaluations and new inflation and so on. Because of this state of instability, the investor must recognize, when the time seems proper, what Thomas Jefferson said, "The merchant has no country."

The Need to Stay Solvent

Once in most generations, and it has been so since civilization began, comes a time when the prudent investor must enter a period of self-examination, a time when every man must act for himself alone. He must forgo some of the insular notions on which he may have been raised, and must read and learn more in order to survive financially. He needs to attain a global concept. For such times, when things are going quite wrong, not only will politicians and others be saying things were never better, but governments will be inflicting more and more controls.

Historically, they introduce controls as a patch job—to keep the system going—because it is awkward to admit (even if they know better) that errors have been made— or that the structure is faulty or the ship of state is off course. *Basic* premises are rarely examined. Government always has to deal with the *urgent*, so it has no time for the *important*. It is the same in our private lives. Hence one must act when the signs are first recognized and do so before controls prevent such individual action.

At a time when the lessons of the last generation have been largely forgotten, usually after an era of prosperity, there comes a moment when things start going askew monetarily or economically, while those in positions of influence proclaim most loudly that things are quite sound. It is especially for such a time that this book is written, to show you the facilities available internationally, when crises make it necessary to rely only on yourself.

This is certainly not a book against anyone or anyplace. To the contrary, it is a book *for* stability and long-term continuity. Indeed it is written in the belief that there are times to take a "holiday" from the one-country concept of investment. It is not a case of leaving a sinking ship but of facing the reality that you are no use to your country or family or yourself if your life's savings are decimated or you become bankrupt.

This book is written in hope that some of you will preserve your capital and be there to "pick up the pieces" for the next generation, so you will be solvent when most people do not have the capital. For in the depths of economic chaos, a country most needs *solvent* citizens for her recovery.

CHAPTER 2

The Philosophy of Sound Currency

"Money speaks sense in a language all nations understand."
Aphra Behn

TO help us recognize when money becomes what it should *not* be, and to understand the principles of value, worth, and numerical-increase, it is well at this stage to define *what* money is and what it should be. It's useful, I think, for us to go back to discover how money came into being and how and why it works.

Why Man Trades

Adam Smith said, "Man is an animal that makes bargains; no other animal does this—no dog exchanges bones with another." In this he summarized a fundamental base of human society. Animals in their wild state are totally free. They depend on no one but themselves for survival. Neither do they accept authority except in minor ways in small family units. Man on the other hand gave up this ultimate form of freedom in favor of prosperity many centuries ago. He discovered there were certain advantages to living in a community.

Ever since that first decision to live in a community he has sought a balance between freedom and security. Man also found that "the whole is greater than the sum of the parts." In other words, if he could produce a pair of shoes, an axe, cooking utensils, and perhaps raise a few cattle he could be self-sufficient, but if he only made shoes and traded those shoes for the other things he needed he could be more prosperous; for he was better at making shoes than raising cattle and so it made more sense to let those who could raise cattle better, do it, and then exchange the end products.

There came a time when straightforward exchange, or barter, became too cumbersome, for if he wished to barter six pairs of shoes for an ox, he not only had to find a man with the right ox, but he had to find a man with the right ox who wanted six pairs of shoes! In other words there had to exist a double coincidence of wants before trading could take place. This brought about the setting of certain "standards." A standard of value had to be established within communities so that prices could then be agreed upon in terms of that standard.

A Standard of Value

The principle of the standard was a thing of recognized generally accepted value, in terms of which all other goods could be "priced." Your six pairs of shoes for example were worth that one ox, and your three bags of wheat were worth two oxen, and so on.

One of the earliest standards was in fact *cattle (pecus* in Latin, whence we get the word pecuniary). Other standards that were used in early times were leather, wool, honey, oil, wine, and of course gold and silver. In early days precious metals were usually exchanged in the form of jewelry and therefore served a double purpose. The best known non-metal standard was the cowrie shell which was used throughout much of the primitive world. In fact when the Japanese invaded New Guinea in 1942 it was still in use; they distributed the shells freely, and a local district official accused them of endangering "the economic and financial stability of the district."

Hence it can be seen that man has accepted throughout history that in order to be able to exchange and yet keep

"I KNOW NOTHING ABOUT ART—I JUST KNOW WHAT I LIKE....."

most of his freedom, it was necessary to establish a money *standard.* These days so many people wage war on gold itself that the basic argument is forgotten. There is nothing magic about gold. Neither does it hold a monopoly in history as a money standard. The issue of gold today is merely that something, regardless of what one chooses, has to regulate the money supply if that supply is to remain of reasonably constant value. Paper money, which *can* be increased at will, inevitably ends up being increased in *just* that manner.

When this happens inflation occurs which shows itself to the ordinary man when he finds that the general price level is rising, and yet his *purchasing* power is falling. If it happens very slowly he probably won't notice, particularly as progress (i.e. better and better products, and cheaper methods to produce these products) helps to counteract his dropping buying power.

But why does inflation happen? Surely anything that can be so disastrous as the type of inflation that much of South America constantly battles with, or that which hit Germany after World War I, would be avoided. Let us examine the causes of inflation.

Causes of Inflation

Wars are one cause, because the amount of taxation needed to make a war possible on a major scale would be totally unacceptable to the population, and so inflation is an easier way of "taxing." Pestilence used to cause it a lot (like the Black Death in 1348) where you suddenly find your population halved and the money supply the same. The interruption of normal supplies to a city can cause inflation, for example in a besieged city, for then the natural supply-demand equation is disturbed and the supply of money stays the same but the supply of goods diminishes. New discoveries of gold and silver have done it in the past, for even gold cannot survive, and would not survive as a standard of value if there were unlimited quantities. This was evident during the discovery era of the Sixteenth Century. New financial methods like the printing and use of bank notes can cause it, and indeed are causing it *today.* Governments now tend to expand the flow of money and credit at a faster rate than the flow of things on which money and credit can be spent are produced.

So what actually happens when this "inflation" hits? It completely upsets the law of supply and demand. It upsets monetary value because the basis of the numerical count of the money is not founded on what is actually happening in the economy but rather on what governments would LIKE to see happen, and in this case unfortunately the wish does NOT become father to the action. It alters legal relationships and social relationships, for society tends to operate on fixed monetary values, with money earned slowly, with a dollar given for a dollar earned. Intelligence and a sense of social responsibility are prone to be in relationship to the wealth of individuals. When this breaks down, then morals are inclined to go too. Value is lost sight of in every area. The wrong things become things demanded, like government subsidy. In fact Keynes once said to his mother that he could double the length of every shopping queue by slipping an extra £ 5 into every pay packet one Friday.

Inflation and Taxation

Inflation also gives a double revenue to governments, not only in the form of hidden taxes (i.e. you receive less in value than you think and the top is skimmed off for government projects), but in countries where there is progressive taxation, it means that as inflation gets worse, and wages go up in an attempt to keep pace, you may not be earning any more (i.e. your purchasing power may not change) but you will suddenly find yourself in a *higher tax bracket*, and therefore subject to more taxation. So until "their sins find them out," inflation is of double benefit to governments.

It would seem that these days one of the main reasons for governments to inflate, is that it enables them to put into practice the "welfare" programs they promised at the elections without having to let the voters see just how costly these schemes are, for inflation isn't seen in the way extra taxes are, and governments have no wealth that the people do not first give them.

Historical Forms of Money

These days the people who advocate Special Drawing Rights, and other forms of increasing the supply of paper, have lost the basic concept of money. Money is only necessary to form a relationship of prices of goods one to another, *not* as an end in itself.

Even when man has been in isolated communities, his need to have a standard of value has always existed. In the adventurer days, out of the realm of civilization, furs, salt, and even opium have been used. In early Australian times rum was used, and in prisoner of war camps cigarettes and Red Cross parcels were used in many cases in exactly the same way as currency.

A Store of Value

So it can be seen, that there is no evidence that paper on its own can ever be a "sound" currency.

Money has to fulfill *two* main functions: to be a *medium of exchange* which those wishing to trade can agree on, and the second (which limits considerably what *can* be used as a yardstick) to be a store of value. In other words, the primitive things like cattle and rum would be hopeless in a modern society because *their* value would fluctuate too much. If a man had no need to spend his rum-money for a year, he wanted to know he could still buy in a year hence what he could buy today. This is one reason why a precious metal makes such a good standard. Its price is naturally relatively stable in the market place.

Slavery and Money

It is interesting to note that there exists a distinct relationship between slavery and money. The decline of the Roman Empire and the collapse of her money threw all

Europe into a form of slavery. The lord-and-serf relationship was nothing more than slavery, which was not broken until the growth of mercantilism (i.e. trade) nearly 1000 years later. The breakdown was also abetted by the growth of nationalism. The wage-earning freeman is the modern version of the serf and marks a decisive step forward in the progress of mankind. You will note that the cry for abolition of slavery a century ago was not against cruelty. The battle cries were not for kinder masters, but for freedom of slaves, and the ONLY way a slave can be free is to be paid in money for his services and be allowed to take that payment away and use it as he pleases. Without that payment he is in bondage, for he has no means to survive except at the will of those who feed him.

In the Middle Ages the serf with a good lord was probably better fed and better housed than the adventurer on the high seas out to make a quick fortune, but one was free and the other was not. Today the trend is towards removing money and paying "in kind." In other words our money is taken (or withheld) in taxes and inflation, and we are given instead goods and services in the form of various welfare programs (subsidies, Social Security, Medicare, etc.). In this sense therefore whole nations are moving towards a master/serf relationship. Socialism is a kind term for a slave-like condition of state and citizen, a sort of benevolent slavery. Socialism is gaining ground in the US, Great Britain, Scandinavia and elsewhere. Some people even welcome this trend. Many serfs I am sure did not envy the adventurer on the high seas. But this book is not written for the man who wants security at the hand of a government or master. It is written for the man who wants freedom at the risk of security, and knows that his money, *if kept free* and *intact* in value, will enable him to have a greater freedom.

The function of *free* trade is and always was a delicate balance between man's desire to obtain the most efficient use out of his world and his reluctance to give up more freedom than was absolutely necessary in order to do this.

Man's ultimate right to decide for *himself* how much of his talent, work, mind, and spirit he is willing to offer other men in return for what he wants and needs is surely his most cherished possession. A *good* currency system recognizes and respects this and allows for it.

Graham Hutton said, "It took all the centuries of humanity's painful advance up to 1914 to achieve democratic representational self-government, universal adult suffrage, and personal freedom. Within half a century after 1914, despite phenomenal material progress which removed real poverty from among Western societies, that achievement was in *retreat* on a worldwide front, threatened by the monstrous regiment of state functionaries."

When To Act Alone

What does he mean? Aside from the social aspect, he means simply that in recent years we have decided we can trust banks and governments to issue IOU's against a money standard, and even to decree the money standard itself. Sometimes it is an honest standard, sometimes it isn't. Sometimes governments get so carried away with themselves on this task that they claim they can do away with the very standard they were designated to write the IOU's against. It is at such times that you have to make a decision. As soon as paper money in your country becomes backed by government decree and little else, it is time to find a safer haven for all or part of your assets. Government decrees can change, and *whatever* they do, automatically makes the currency unstable, for money is most stable when allowed to price itself in a free market.

ALL government control makes for instability over the long term. It is at such times the prudent man must act alone.

On Prognosticators

Some may say: "But I know a man who has been predicting disaster for the last ten years and if I had listened then I would have made a lot less than I have today." This does happen. However, there are two points here: *1.* You should do your *own* thinking, and not blame someone else for not making a perfect prediction. The art of using economic predictions is to weigh the premises on which the prognosticators have MADE the prediction, not just take the prediction on blind faith. *2.* Many prognosticators ARE right in fact; it is merely their timing that is sometimes off. There is a good reason for this. Sometimes people expect perfection in an imperfect world and the world is *never* perfect.

Even in eras of national greatness there is a lot of "wrong." In fact if one looks back and examines the stupidities of government and social structure one wonders at the fact that it holds together at all. This is where many prognosticators err in timing. There are two schools, the one which says that as society *can* hold together in spite of any underlying chaos, it can do it permanently; these people tend to be permanent Bulls. The other school is the one that sees things going quite wrong, but that underestimates how much society can take BEFORE it falls apart. These people tend to take perfection as the norm and work away from that, instead of taking a lot less than perfection as their base. This tends to put their timing off by a number of months or in some cases years. But they are usually right in the end. In spite of the error in timing the second group of people are in many ways more sound and pragmatic, for it is surely better to survive relatively affluent and never have made the extra millions than to have seen the multi-millions made on paper only to lose them fast, and end up bankrupt.

On Politicians

We live our lives by legislation and decisions hammered out by men in smoke-filled rooms, often men who have been up all night, who are far too busy being public relations men (they can't help it; it's the System) to be able to have really done their homework on the subject on which they are making the decision. Then at 5 A.M. someone says, "God I'm tired, let's do it Sam's way and go home." The momentous decision is made.

However, as humans we appear to endure and live with a state of mild chaos. It is only when the mild chaos becomes major chaos that trouble starts. But how do we know it is getting critical? Probably the best rule of thumb is an old British adage: "Never believe anything political unless it is officially denied." When politicians start making unsolicited statements that the currency is strong and the economy is vigorous then it's probably time to find a new home for your money.

Act Before the End

You will probably be too early, speaking in general. But in this game three years too early is better than an hour too late, and the chances are that restrictions will be clamped on to prevent the movement of capital long before the final fiasco has been reached. Speaking in the specific, 1970 is no longer too early. It is perhaps (for this cycle) just barely in time, before the gates are shut.

However, you will be in a small minority. In times of economic chaos, most people go under. So in order to survive you have to question everything, and not mind ridicule. It is never pleasant to leave the party after the second drink when everybody else is having fun, just because you sense trouble. They will laugh at you, call you old-fashioned, and will go on deprecating you right up to the time the police arrive to break up the party.

At such times governments have many "tools" or weapons at their disposal. They make endless "official" statements claiming all is well. They "seasonally adjust" the various economic statistics in new ways. They lower the official backing for the currency to make it look as if nothing has changed. They make a moral issue out of your prudence, and they call names and create Cassandras out of those who run for protective cover. They damn the principles they once embraced. What was once revered is made illegal.

In the *final* stages, politicians slap on tighter controls, make individual judiciousness (in various forms) a criminal offense, and make it nearly impossible for anybody to go against the government, on the pseudo-patriotic basis that if *they* go *everybody* goes with them.

Hence you must act BEFORE the end of such cycles or waves in human behavior. The waves are as predictable as the tides—in human terms.

CHAPTER 3

Some Historical Examples

"There is no subtler, nor surer, means of overturning the existing basis of society than to debauch the currency. The process engages all the hidden forces of the economic law on the side of destruction, and does it in a manner which not one man in a million is able to diagnose." John Maynard Keynes, *Economic Consequences of Peace.*

IN order to show the chaos that can be caused by governments, albeit often well meaning, I hope in this chapter to briefly outline some of the monetary collapses of history, to show how it happens stage by stage, for you will see that they all have a great deal in common. I also hope to show how it is necessary to act well BEFORE a monetary holocaust ignites, because even the day before it arrives is too late.

Governments all seem to follow a pattern, and indeed the whole cycle of debauching the currency is very similar everywhere it happens.

The pattern followed goes something like this. First we have a relatively sound currency. Then, *not* for lack of economic prosperity, but to curry public favor, politicians offer *greater* prosperity (with government help). Those in power feel they are "forced" to inflate to mask a strain on the system. They also raise taxes but most tax is hidden in the form of inflation, because the full amount of money needed (to provide whatever service they've promised) would not be an acceptable amount to take openly from the voters.

Unfortunately the error in this does not show itself immediately. Indeed it can take years of "managed money"

for the whole thing to topple, by which time the managers
are so pleased with their management that they can't believe there was anything fundamentally wrong in the first
place. New leaders may have replaced older ones who
don't even know (or care, or question) how it began. They
just accept.

So when the first cracks in the dam appear, their in-
stincts lead them to "more of the same" rather than a
rectification of the original wrong. This of course has the
same effect as taking a drug. By not attempting a with-
drawal process at the first signs that health is affected, and
by increasing the dosage, ultimately the patient dies. So it
is with an economy.

I am not necessarily suggesting by this list of cautionary
tales of the past, that the USA or any other major nation
will shortly go down the precise path of any of the past
disasters. On the contrary, I would say that it is quite
possible that fortunately the disaster may come *earlier*
(and thus be less severe) in the cycle, largely because of the
new factor today of intensive communication. It's rather
like the new techniques that make it possible to discover
cancer at an early stage; it is thus less likely to be fatal.

However, I am prepared to admit that the monetary
debacle will be bad enough to warrant drastic action. And
certainly the time for you to act is well before the event.
The reason is that when governments start believing that
"more of the same" will *cure*, they invariably also add
controls to prevent any of their citizens disagreeing with
their methods. Therefore long before the storm hits, citizens find themselves KNOWING things are going wrong
but finding that because of government control they have
to let their personal savings go down with the mistakes of
the country's politicians. So act before your government
gets desperate.

In seeking precise comparisons between the past and the USA today, we find at least two countries (or civilizations if you prefer) where a close parallel can be drawn. As the dollar is a kind of currency standard for countries outside its own boundaries, we sought like circumstances. Before the US, probably only the currencies of Rome and Great Britain had roles so nearly like the dollar.

Pax Romana

Until the present, and we all hope that even 50 years from now this fact will still be true, Roman currency suffered the *longest* progressive inflation of any money anywhere. This was the *basic* reason why Rome fell. It directly caused the Dark Ages, with its feudal society yoke. So it can be said that while the Roman inflation lasted through a number of generations, the depression (both social and economic) that followed lasted for *a thousand years.* Imagine a depression of that length! A depression where society crumbled to a point where many inventions were destroyed and had to wait a millennium to be reconstructed!

Hence it can be said that, with history as an example, far from centralized economic management *creating* prosperity, rather if allowed to run long enough government management can not only destroy prosperity, it can destroy what man has invented. It literally DOES kill the goose that lays the golden egg. Only man's inventiveness can create prosperity. Government need only create a free market climate.

Following *all* downfalls comes what we call "a return to moral values," which in terms of the little depressions we know, of 2–3 years, is perhaps a good thing. But if the prior inflation is too severe then the overcompensating reaction can almost destroy man, as anything more than a noncreative animal, for decades or even centuries, as happened when the whole known world was thrown into dictatorship on a provincial level which created for man a world easily as rigid and narrow, both mentally and physically, as anything in Russia today. But how did it all happen? How did the people who inhabited those cities we now view with wonder, with running water and a type of modern plumbing, literally go back to mud huts?

First, the state's expenditure became intolerably burdensome. They were protecting a vast frontier which was far away from their own immediate lands. Bureaucracy had grown. Civil administration, law and transport had become a state responsibility. They performed a sort of nationalization on more and more areas of trade. Even more jobs became hereditary thus reducing the possibility of advancement by ability and destroying incentive. Taxes went up and up until, as Nero said, "Let's see to it that nobody owns anything."

The need to keep the proletariat-voters happy made for the ever increasing requirement for "bread and circuses." When Rome finally fell, it fell from *within*. The barbarians wanted to capture it, not destroy it. But just as today if an army of uncivilized African bushmen took over Moscow, then the whole structure of the USSR would fall. So it did in Rome. How different from that same African army, say, capturing Berne. If they did so, then the rest of Switzerland would go on more or less as before. The difference is economic independence *within* the state.

But this is a long time ago, you say. True, but when one thinks that it was basically inflation that canceled out a thousand years of development and put man's progress back as if it had never happened, then although it happened a long time ago, its repercussions are felt even today; for who knows how much further advanced we would be had Rome never fallen and the graph of man's progress had gone steadily upwards? Furthermore, "The more things change the more they remain the same." So no matter how long ago Rome fell, the emotional pattern of human behavior doesn't change—and this is what causes man to repeat his mistakes.

As it is, it took man until the beginning of the Twentieth Century to *again* reach representative self-government and personal freedom and a mechanized society. Yet having once more achieved such heights of civilization, the trend since then has been again towards managed currencies, and more government-fostered centralization.

Indeed countries have collapsed *because* of managed money and inflation in *this* century. The main difference between most of them and Rome is that they did not rule most of the known world as Rome did, and so they could not force inflation almost indefinitely, as Rome did. Let us look first at the bad inflation in France at the end of the Eighteenth and beginning of the Nineteenth Century.

France

It was in 1789 that the French found themselves in debt, and as always a short road to prosperity was sought. However, they were still hurting from the wild plans of John Law, decades before. So they decided that this time it would be different. They concluded that paper money under despotism was dangerous and fostered corruption, and that was why the John Law fiasco had happened, but that paper money under constitutional government was very different and there was no danger. They backed their money with Church *land* which was taken over for this purpose and which was about *one quarter* of the entire real property in France, valued at two billion livres.

Their first plan was only to issue bills too large to be used as ordinary currency, and bills which would bear interest and so encourage their hoarding. However, in order to have something to pay out immediately it was decided to issue four hundred million paper currency notes in both small and large bills in order to stimulate business. They deceived themselves by saying that if any nation could safely issue paper money, France could, as she had learned from the John Law episode; and now she had a constitutional government, controlled by enlightened patriotic people, and every livre was secured by a virtual mortgage of land.

Of course they would not make the same mistakes as John Law had. He had bankrupted all of France 68 years prior as Comptroller General. In the final year of his fiasco the gold Louis coin had gone from 45 livres in value to 20,000 livres. The generation that had made those mistakes was gone.

It was said of this new land-backed currency: "These assignats, bearing interest as they do, will soon be considered better than the coin now hoarded, and will bring it out again into circulation." (Sound familiar?)

The result of this issue was success. A portion of public debt was paid, credit revived, trade increased. Had they stopped right there, it might have been a good idea. However, as always happens, five months after the first issue times grew difficult again. Obviously, they said, if the first issue had been such a success the answer was to issue more. In September 1790 a bill was passed to issue eight hundred million more new assignats, but they accompanied the bill with a solemn declaration that in no case should the entire amount put in circulation exceed twelve hundred millions. By this time, small silver and copper money had disappeared from circulation, and there was much fraud. Different districts of France started to issue their own assignats in small denominations, and this caused the National Assembly to evade the twelve million limit. Within a short time one hundred and sixty million livres in paper had been received into the treasury, and much of it was reissued as smaller notes. About this time citizens were being spurred to send their silverware and jewels to the mint. The King sent gold and silver plate and churches were required by law to send in all gold and silver not absolutely essential for public worship. (Governments have made this demand on citizens since history began. Franklin D. Roosevelt requested citizens to turn in gold coin in 1934, as did Hitler in 1937.)

But silver and copper continued to "disappear." In November 1790 a coinage standard of silver was tried, but in vain, and it was found necessary to issue another hundred million notes. Prices were rising fast, and the pressure for more circulating medium (i.e. liquidity) grew more intense. The French now believed that inflation was prosperity, and clamored for more notes. However, as each new issue came out there was a marked depreciation. This was excused as simply due to lack of knowledge and confidence among the rural population, and it was proposed to issue a statement showing them the soundness of the currency and the absurdity of preferring coin. But specie (metallic money) disappeared more and more.

By January 1791 newspapers were declaring that the whole thing was the fault of speculators who were drawing money off to Germany. I can't help it if much of this sounds more like 1969 than 1791. The newspapers said the English were issuing propaganda against paper. Murders of "unpatriotic criminals" were not rare. Although money was increasing, prosperity was diminishing and business started to stagnate. Heavy duties were put on foreign goods to "help" home manufacturers.

By the end of 1791 money could lose up to 40% of its value in a month. Existence became hand to mouth. By this time public speakers were declaring that a depreciated currency was a good thing, and that gold and silver were an unsatisfactory method of measuring value, and how it was good that currency could not go out of the country. By July 1792 twenty-four hundred million paper currency livres were in circulation, and a decree was passed to issue three hundred million more.

During all this monetary inflation, prices had risen beyond belief but wages stayed largely where they were four years before. It reminds us that Daniel Webster said, "Of all the contrivances for cheating the laboring classes of mankind, none has been more effective than that which deludes them with paper money."

By December 1792 thirty-five hundred million had been circulated, of which six hundred million had been withdrawn. In 1793 however, another source of wealth was available to the government, the confiscation of the large estates of the landed proprietors who had by this time fled the country. Historically a great many of the "better" people leave a country when it's too far gone to save. On this land money was issued until three billion were in circulation. However, the journey of the currency was not *always* down, which helped to delude the public. It *fluctuated*, sometimes as much as 10%. By now the starving peasants were saying it was all the shopkeepers' fault and by murdering them the problem would be solved. This and other similar possibilities of solution increased the activity of the guillotine.

In 1793 it was decreed that anybody selling gold or silver coin or making any difference in any transaction between paper and specie would be imprisoned in irons for six years for the first offense. A reward was offered to informers. In May 1794 a sentence of *death* was passed on anybody "having asked before a bargain was concluded, in *what money* payment was to be made." In November 1793 it became a criminal offense with terrifying penalties to trade in gold or silver. In August 1794 a law was passed making the selling of paper currency at a discount punishable by twenty years' imprisonment, and making *foreign* investments by Frenchmen punishable by death.

But in spite of all the government tried to do, the "louis d'or" (gold Louis coin) stood in the market place registering the true value of the currency. On August 1, 1795, this gold Louis of 25 francs was worth 920 paper francs. On September 1, its value was 1200 francs; on November 1st, 2600 francs; and in February 1796 it rose to 7200 francs. Throughout this period all prices were enormously inflated, EXCEPT THE PRICE OF WAGES. As far back as 1794 a "crawling peg" or "table of depreciation" was talked about, but it was abandoned. The end result was the total collapse of France, financially, morally, and politically. It was a collapse that only a Napoleon could retrieve. And retrieve he did for, as he wrote to his minister: "While I live I will never resort to irredeemable paper."

Germany

Now to this century. Prior to 1914 the German mark contained .398 grams of gold and was worth 23.8 US cents. In 1913 paper circulation was a little over 5 billion, with 2 billion of gold in the treasury. But by 1918 money supply was *70 billion* and the mark was pegged at an unreal price (because of wartime controls) of 17.18 US cents. Germany issued emergency money before the official signing of the peace treaty, made of zinc, iron, brass, aluminum, glazed cardboard, and paper, the idea being that it would be redeemed on the signing of the peace treaty.

However, the conditions of peace in terms of reparations were ruthless and disrupted Germany's internal economic balance. Hence after the treaty large issues of interest-bearing bonds were floated. Soon there ceased to be a *market* for bonds. So currency was issued, and more currency, and more currency, while the real wealth of Germany was sucked out under the terms of the Versailles peace treaty. By the end of 1923 there were a little under 500,000,000,000,000,000,000 marks in circulation and the rate was quoted *hourly*.

By the end of 1923 wholesale prices were 1,400,000,-000,000 times as high as in 1913. The price of a newspaper was 200,000,000,000 marks. German bankers, however, bought bundles of marks. They simply did not *believe* the currency could become worthless. On August 30th, 1924, the Reichsmark was introduced on an exchange rate of 1 new Reichsmark equal to 1,000,000,000,000 old marks. It had the same gold value as the old mark. The national debt was marked down to 2½ to 5 cents on the dollar. Mortgages were reduced to 25% of face value. Industrial bonds to 15%. Later when the German devaluation occurred in 1948 after W.W.II, the mark was internally devalued at the rate of 100 Reichsmarks to 6 Deutschmarks.

The German people learned about inflation the hard way. It robbed them of their middle class, that class of bourgeois leaders, independently minded because of being a property-owning class, and yet loyal to state and society. Because of this it left the country virtually leaderless and made it easier for a Hitler to take over. It took a Dr. Erhard to end the second inflation after World War II with his economic miracle.

Illustrated here is one of the catastrophes or mishaps in US currency, most of which occurred in the 18th and 19th centuries. These continental notes, like many others, were totally repudiated by the government within a few years and the phrase "not worth a continental" still reminds us of them today.

The Decline and Fall of the British Empire

In the years prior to World War I, the British citizen had watched British powers spread around the globe, and seen fresh technical marvels introduced every year; he had no reason to doubt that this would continue and that Britain

In 1922–3, mark notes were printed in larger denominations
as the months rolled by. In October 1923, this 200,000,000,000
mark note was put in circulation. In August 1924, the new
Reichsmark was introduced with an exchange rate of 1 Reichsmark equal to 1,000,000,000,000 marks.

HUNGARIAN PENGO
The 1,000,000,000 pengo note issued in 1946 is worth $175,-
000,000 based on the 1939 value of the pengo. However, due
to wild inflation, it has no monetary value whatever today.

would continue to head this march of improvement. But
even prior to the war there were certain weaknesses to be
seen. Britain had been the herald of the industrial revolution and was already being a little overtaken in her methodry by newer industrial nations. Little enough, but even
this was to be noticed in her increasing loss of competitive
edge.

Then came war. Taxes shot up and this, combined with inflation, took the direct taxation yield from £ 94 million in 1913–14 to £ 721 million in 1919–20. Inflation was adopted as government policy. In place of the pre-war bank notes backed by a highly sensitive gold reserve there were now currency notes created by the Treasury in denominations of £ 1 and 10 shillings. They were to have been issued to the banks as a loan at current bank rate, to aid them in staving off the expected run on their deposits, but since no run developed and the banks were unwilling to pay interest on loans they did not require, the Treasury issued these notes freely to the public.

The direct inflationary effect however was quite small. The value of the notes in circulation rose from £ 35 million in 1914 to a peak of £ 354 in 1920, after which it declined, but to some extent the notes were replacing gold which had either been withdrawn or gone into hiding. Hence it can be said that for the period of the war at any rate, inflation as policy was to allow the war to be financed, but this of course took its toll of prices and the cost of living.

War finished with wholesale prices 140% and cost of living 120% above the level of July 1914. Technically deflation might have been possible in 1919, but politically it was unthinkable. As the soldiers returned, the fear was of widespread unemployment, not runaway inflation. Instead of restricting credit, Britain formally went off the gold standard in March 1919.

On this swelling of easy credit, employment picked up and the pent-up demand for goods was given full rein, so prices shot up. Hence the "boom" of 1919–20 was pure inflation. Prices climbed but production at no point came anywhere near that of 1913. In April 1920 the government took fright and introduced a deflationary budget. The decline came fast, with unemployment rising from 2% to 18% and business activity falling from 117.9 to 90.0 in one year.

Some months before this deflationary policy there were voices in the wilderness for a return to a gold standard, and the re-establishment of the "safety of the Bank of England" when London controlled the credit markets of the world. The voices gathered more strength until finally in April 1925 the gold standard was re-imposed. It failed miserably. Not because there was anything wrong with a gold standard, but because England had had gold priced the same for so long that it never occurred to anybody that to re-tie gold to the pound might just mean changing the *price* of gold in the process. Deflation, ruthless as it had been, had not been enough to bring prices and the economy back to pre-World War I levels and so the pound, tied to the pre-war gold price, was pegged at least 10% too high in the international markets. All because they regarded the gold price as *inviolate.* Sound familiar?

The pound fluctuated as much as a dollar during the early Twenties on the foreign exchange market, and by re-tying back to pre-war gold, England attempted to fix the pound at a $4.86 rate instead of $4.45 which would have been more realistic. But England was stuck. Industry probably wouldn't take any more cuts in wages without industrial violence. Even so, the attempt to return to pre-war gold, considering the weakness of British economy after the war, was in itself an achievement, and the act, though failing at home, did much to contribute to stabilization of foreign exchanges.

Of course one of the biggest antagonists of the return to gold in this period was John Maynard Keynes. His fears proved correct, but for the wrong reasons. All that was wrong, and which caused problems until the 1929 crisis, was simply the return to a *pre-war* pound; it was simply overvalued. The beginning of the end for England had begun. The first World War had killed her greatness, and the second World War was the final blow to an already tottering empire.

American Money

But some may say that while these accounts act as cautionary tales, they have not happened in the USA. So perhaps we should spend a little time examining the history of American money. Few seem to know it.

As in many primitive civilizations, the early Americans floundered about searching for a standard of value. European coinage was in short supply, so they used other standards like beaver skins, tobacco, rice, and of course wampum. In 1640 the colony of Massachusetts set a value on white beaded Indian belts at fourpence, to be used as trading currency. In 1641 the beads were made lawful money for any sum under £ 10.

In other words, lacking a metallic standard of value, the early colonists did *not* just create money, they adopted the "money" of their Indian neighbors. The use of money extended as far south as Virginia. In 1691 tobacco was made legal tender in Virginia, and in order to stabilize it as a backing in terms of English currency it was put under public warehousing. In 1727 notes redeemable in tobacco were made legal tender. As well as these odd forms of money, English and other foreign money also circulated.

However, came the revolutionary war and governments of the colonies needed great amounts of money. At this time the Spanish silver "piece of eight" was in reasonable supply, having been received in large quantities in the Southern states as payment of tobacco.

The Continental Congress assembled at Philadelphia decided to issue paper notes promising to pay the bearer

"Spanish Milled Dollars according to the Resolution of the Congress, held in Philadelphia the 10th day of May 1775." On either side was printed "Continental Currency" —thus the US formally departed from the British system of coinage. This resolution was confirmed by Congress in 1785.

By the end of the war, however, so many of the "Continentals" had been printed (both by Congress and by forgers) that the "promises to pay" could not be met in any coin, let alone Spanish milled dollars. So the US first real attempt at centralized paper money was a total disaster which is still remembered today in the phrase "Not worth a Continental."

Since the Continental paper money went out of circulation as useless, business again became dependent on English, French, and Portuguese coins. The different coins made trade difficult, and of course they got themselves exported to pay for imported goods. By 1785 the new country was in the throes of depression, and as expected the cry went up for paper money. The cry was resisted after the prior fiasco, but only after a struggle, for the lives of legislators in New Hampshire were threatened unless the demand for paper was met, and the militia had to be called to disperse the crowds. Western Massachusetts revolted in favor of more paper and had to be put down by the Army.

In 1792 the first Bank of the United States issued its first currency on the strength of Congress. The new dollar was defined as 24.75 grains of gold. In the belief that a grain of gold was equal to 15 grains of silver it was provided that a silver dollar should contain 24.75 times 15 or 371.25 grains of pure silver. Free and unlimited coinage of gold and silver was provided for. This was not particularly successful for gold was exported in great amounts. However,

owing to Europe being plunged into war soon after adop-
tion of the American Constitution, Hamiltonian economics appeared much sounder than they were, for young
America was to start a trend of turning European wars to
her advantage and was able to find new markets and
launch the Constitution on a wave of prosperity.

When the Charter for the first US bank expired, the
conservatives would not renew it. With the loss of the
restraining hand of a specie bank, numerous state banks
sprang up. Their various notes circulated at discounts
sometimes up 50 percent.

Then came the War of 1812 which the government
financed mainly by loans and these were soon selling at
20% discount. After the disastrous fiscal experience of this
war, the conservatives changed their minds and chartered
a second US bank. The first three years were again disastrous but in 1819 the bank was restored to soundness and
until 1828 was functioning effectively. However, after that
its power was used unscrupulously to play politics, and the
1832 presidential election used the bank as a political issue. The Democrats won, which was doom to the bank.

Thanks to the natural function of Gresham's Law, gold
disappeared and only silver dollars were left. These were
discontinued in 1806 (to create scarcity) in an attempt to
force a de-hoarding of gold. In 1834 the official ratio of
gold to silver was changed to 16-1 in the hope this would
alleviate the situation. Also the weight of the gold dollar
was reduced to 23.22 grains, the weight of the silver dollar
remaining the same. Under this new government-ordained
ratio, gold was overvalued, and therefore gold reappeared
and silver disappeared.

The discovery of gold in California in 1848 made gold
even more overvalued. During this time an increasing
number of bank notes were being issued by state banks.

These notes were of varying soundness, and penalties were enacted on banks which failed to redeem their notes, but counterfeiting was common and penalties in most cases were virtually unenforceable.

A crop failure in 1835 set off a panic which four years later forced every bank in the country to suspend specie payment. This was made much worse by the heavy debt incurred from abroad and local speculation. Recovery was made and again excess speculation triggered panic in 1857.

The Civil War

The financial effect of the Civil War was unbelievable. At the outbreak of war the South owed Northern merchants $300,000,000, most of which had literally to be written off as bad debt. Uncertainty as to the future directly brought on the depression of 1861. Banks had far too few reserves to meet an emergency and in that same year 6000 failures of Northern firms, for sums of $5000 or more, were reported, plus many below that amount.

In the latter part of December 1861, the Northern banks suspended specie payment, followed almost at once by the federal government. In the South with the exception of New Orleans, specie payment was suspended at the outbreak of war and was continued until the end. Needless to say the wildcat banks of the then even wilder West were especially hard hit and along with them of course their depositors.

Confederate Money

When war broke out the Southern states were in debt to both the North and Europe, so no more loans were forthcoming. The government of the Confederacy up to 1863 endeavored to support itself with bond issues and fiat money in the form of treasury notes (of which about one billion dollars was issued).

With only the credit of the Confederate government behind them, the treasury notes speedily depreciated until February 17, 1864, when the Confederacy passed an act for either the compulsory funding of all notes into 4% bonds or the exchange of all notes under $100 for new notes at the rate of three old for two new. During this time one gold dollar would purchase 61 Confederate paper dollars. This action drove people back to barter for the rest of the war.

The North

During the four years of the Civil War, government expenditure was more than the whole previous history of the USA. To support this a tariff tax, the usual way of obtaining tax money then, was raised to 47 percent. Also, an income tax was levied for the first time in U.S. history in 1861 at 3%, which was soon raised to 10% on all incomes over $5000. The tax was not abolished until 1872. In 1865 public debt reached a high point that was not surpassed until 1917. Another method which helped finance the war was the issuance of notes based "on the credit of the United States." (Sound familiar?)

By 1862 there were a little under 2000 banks, each issuing currency which circulated at a discount and which reflected confidence in the individual bank. Up to this point there was no national currency, so the question of devaluation, etc. did not exist. You put your savings with the bank of your choice and unless you chose very well, you either lost everything when the bank closed and went out of business, or you lost a portion when their bills sold at a discount. In those days the best way to keep the value of your assets was gold coins in your own possession . . . provided of course you could keep from being robbed.

In 1863 the creation of a National Banking System put U.S. currency on a nationwide basis. No longer was it possible, as a bank, to print unlimited notes and then try to circulate them as far as possible away from the owner bank. Stability, at least of sorts, had arrived. At least now there were the greenbacks. However, for many long years a struggle raged to cope with the aftermath of an ineptly financed war.

During the war, textiles quadrupled in price, flour doubled, and meat, fuel and rents increased 50 percent. As in all inflations wages lagged far behind. For the 30 years following the war, the battle was waged by the debtor groups to try to keep prices at war levels to enable them to pay back the same value that had existed when they had contracted the debts. After the war, however, the government started to contract the paper money in circulation. This saw a general decline in prices until about 1879 when a gold standard was re-established.

On an international level the gold standard was more steadily recognized. In fact in 1874 one of the most remarkable coins in all history was minted. It was a gold coin struck by the US Mint and inscribed as follows: "$10, £ 2.1.1., Marken 41.90, Kronen 37.33, Guilden 20.73, Francs 51.81." The right of traders to exchange gold freely from country to country made it a true international standard.

Currency Act of 1900

This at long last, after a century of a *very* checkered career, defined the dollar at 25.8 grains of gold and decreed that all other forms of currency should be maintained at parity with this gold dollar. Gold reserve requirements were established. However, the gold reserve requirement was very small relative to the currency in circulation, being $150,000,000 in gold behind $346,000,-000 greenbacks, $484,000,000 silver certificates, $76,000,-000 coined silver, $331,000,000 bank notes backed by only USA credit. But somehow the parity thus established then survived until 1934 when it was officially changed. But it DID remain, partly at any rate, because new gold was discovered in South Africa, Yukon, and Alaska.

The Twentieth Century

This century to date has been far more stable in the USA than the last. This is partly because she has not been as depleted by war as she was in the century before, and as Europe has been in this century. But it has not been without its problems, the main ones being: 1. The devaluation of the American dollar to 59.06% of its former value in 1934. 2. Two bad periods of inflation—1915 to 1920 when food prices doubled in a little more than four years and 1941 to 1947 when again food prices doubled in just over four years. Since the late 1950's and especially currently inflation has once more become America's chief monetary concern. But this is recent history and will be dealt with in a later chapter.

Middle East and South America

Today if one wishes to examine at first hand the effects of inflation and political instability, then one should visit South America and the Middle East. In much of South America inflation and devaluation, to the tune of twice or more a year, is a way of life. This monetary instability not only creates a general social instability, but has held back industrial progress in South America in a way nothing else could. Interest rates in many places are quoted at something like 20% which at first sounds marvelous, but then you must consider it is the only way people can hope to come out even on devaluations.

In the Middle East it is their politically unstable governments rather than inflation that causes people to put money in Swiss banks. A government-run money system that can be overthrown along with the government can never be trusted. When you go to Geneva you feel as if you have already entered the Middle East.

Conclusion

The study of past inflations is fascinating, and obviously we cannot cover even a fraction of them here. But as stated at the beginning of the chapter they all tend to follow a similar pattern. It is merely the "actor" and the degree that change. Therefore, if any basic rules can be made, when should one act? Oh, that we could pinpoint the day; but human nature being what it is, it is impossible. Also, governments have a permanent policy of clouding the issue. They also deny that anything is wrong right up until the minute they devalue, or close banks, or set up restrictions. They say they do it to prevent "panic" which could worsen the crisis they know is already brewing. This makes it very hard on the man trying to save his life's savings. The main rule which can be made is that as soon as it appears that inflation, government controls, and restrictions are accelerating, then one should take action. If history proves anything it proves that governments cannot be counted on to protect your assets. Indeed they will often seize your assets to protect their jobs. The cynical proverb that fits this then is: "Let's pull together men; every man for himself."

How Much Inflation?

A country can live for a number of years with a 3 percent per annum inflation, even though one might disagree with the whole premise of inflation. Once inflation moves above three percent then an acceleration has begun which is highly dangerous. There is no sure way of knowing at what rate of inflation values will return, or indeed if the thing will collapse under its own runaway course, or if government will finally see the light and act before the end, thus eliminating part of the disaster, or at least lessening its blow. But there are no free rides (i.e. without paying a penalty).

An inflation in its most serious form can *devastate* a country in a way that war never does, for the effects are deeper and much farther reaching. The text book example of this is Germany in this century. She lost World War I, and was partly shell-cratered. The ensuing inflation made it possible for a Hitler to take over. Twenty years later, with no real postwar prosperity to look back on, her leader had brought her to the brink of another war after two decades of privation. In World War II she was devastated *far* worse than in World War I (in fact very little of consequence was left standing). Yet thanks to a strict *monetary* policy, by Erhard, twenty years later Germany has emerged with the strongest economy in Europe.

After wars are over, people work with a will to pick up the pieces. But monetary collapse demoralizes a people and destroys their social structure, which in turn makes them lose their identity in the community. This, like a lingering illness, has no clear-cut end, and is far slower to return to health.

CHAPTER 4

How All This Applies Today

"The way to crush the bourgeoisie is to grind them between the millstones of taxation and inflation."   Lenin

"All the perplexities, confusion and distress in America arise, not from defects in their constitution or confederation; not from want of honor virtue, so much as from downright ignorance of the nature of coin, credit and circulation."   John Adams, 1829

IN the last chapter we saw how inflation and monetary upheaval in the past destroyed economies and how even the USA has experienced them. As mentioned in Chapter One, during the Thirties in the US one could have lost quite a bit through *deflation*, devaluation, and business recession as well.

Modern History

But how does this apply today? What are the signs, if any, that are manifesting themselves now? Are we at a point when moving money abroad might be a good idea, or are the previous cautionary tales merely a warning of what *could* happen? Let us examine the evidence.

In 1945 Congress reduced the gold reserve requirements on both deposits and Federal Reserve notes to 25%, which in itself was an unnecessary inflationary act. Next came massive foreign aid, more or less unrestrained, unrealistic, and disproportionate. This gave an illusion of prosperity in the US and helped push wages so high the US became uncompetitive. Today she faces a crushing balance of payments *deficit*—and (after government-subsidized trade is deducted) an increasing trade deficit as well.

In March 1965 Congress removed the gold reserve requirements on deposits, and in the same year enacted the Coinage Act removing statutory obligation for the Treasury to redeem silver certificates in silver coins.

By March 1968 monetary discipline had deteriorated so far that not only did Congress remove the gold reserve requirement on federal reserve notes, but the free gold market was set up.

Sound familiar? Feel you have read this before in earlier chapters? With backing to currency diminished, and having nothing more to remove, there now began a series of gimmicks which included bank swaps, Roosa bonds, and the infamous Special Drawing Rights which are only indirectly linked to gold. The basic rules of the diminishing backing, and the "need" for government to create money at will, form the same pattern of all inflations since man first invented money.

Gold

It is thirty-five years since America stopped her own citizens trading in gold freely at any price and now she has had virtually to give up the fixed gold price of 35 dollars per ounce.

Since *admitting* this would be tantamount to a dollar devaluation, the two-tier system was set up by which the *official* rate is still 35 dollars and the major central banks agree to deal at this rate. The US will only supply gold to these banks at the fixed rate, or at least that is how the theory goes. But analyst J.F. Smith's description is more accurate of the system as it is in fact practiced: "Instead of calling this a devaluation it is called a two-tier system on the pretense that the official book figure of 35 dollars is still a price even though (virtually) no gold is sold to anyone at that rate."

All other gold is called non-monetary gold and can be bought and sold (by the citizens of those countries permitting it) at the so-called free market price. In fact this too is a farce. The US Treasury, having previously (and strenuously) persuaded other countries to hold dollars rather than trade them in for gold, now not only manages to pressure central bankers not to ask for gold at the official price, but also tries to get as much gold (other people's) sold on the free market as possible so as to hold that price down. A case in point here was the US refusal, for two years, to buy (or let IMF buy) South African gold at 35 dollars an ounce in the hope that this would force it onto the free market. The US seems to have had some limited success here, but it only served to leave the situation unresolved. It postponed solution, which has been US Treasury policy for years. In December 1969 the Rome Agreement ended the US siege and substituted a kind of arms-length blockade. But it proved how frightened US Treasury men were of gold out of chains—and it proved the US lacked power to dictate golden rules to Europe. It also told us time was running out.

Great Britain

Great Britain has the same sort of problems. She has huge debts abroad which originated during World War II and have been added to ever since by borrowing abroad (so as to be able to support the parity of the pound sterling at home). Her reserves are pitifully small and could not begin to pay off all her overseas debts—so a run on the pound, for any reason, tends to rock the international boat. Many countries have staked their savings on the system set up at Bretton Woods and have felt they must be very tolerant of the UK's economic problems. These allies have endlessly lent money (or refrained from withdrawing their reserves) in the hope that Great Britain would put her house in order and that the crumbling fabric of the international monetary system would survive.

Not least of these loans was the much publicized Basel Agreement in 1968 (if it can be called an agreement, for no one will show documentation on anything reportedly agreed) by which huge sums were ostensibly put at Britain's disposal. They were in practice a loan privilege to pay off currency claims at best and at worst they were little more than an expensive public relations smokescreen. The confidence that this bought was fleeting and it only took another month of bad trade figures to bring back the old gloom (and a lower pound price).

We have finally reached the point where people are beginning to realize that loans only worsen a bad situation and put off the reckoning for a few more months or weeks. The UK and the US are virtually bankrupt and this despite the 1967 devaluation which was supposed to set the pound back on its feet. Those countries which hold a large part of their reserves in pounds and dollars are realizing that their hard-earned savings may soon be reduced again unless a solution is found and so they frantically meet time and again to discuss the situation, but with no visible success as yet.

Basic Economic Forces

Each time there is failure to find a permanent solution another loan or gimmick has to be found to support the parities of key currencies, and each one gives yet another gasping space to be followed by yet another crisis. Moving from crisis to crisis like a rudderless ship, one can almost hear the shadowy voice of Abe Lincoln in the background saying, "If we could first know where we are and whither we are tending, we could better judge what to do, and how to do it."

It is surprising that most people have not yet paused to wonder whether we might be walking in the wrong direction, whether we are perhaps mistaking sand for rock. When you are looking for an address and cannot find the way, you ask somebody; but after asking the way ten times and never finding their directions to be correct, you begin to question the understanding of the informants. One wonders when the people of the Free World are going to begin to question the information.

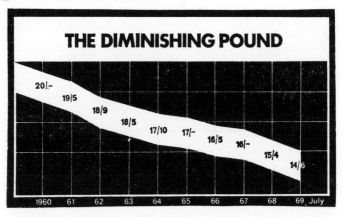

Our governments are fighting *against* basic economic forces and wonder why they do not win. After World War II each currrency was given a fixed price *vis à vis* gold and *vis à vis* each other, i.e. the value of goods and services in each country was fixed *vis à vis* those in all other countries and exchange rates were the rates at which trade could take place. Now it would have been very clever if all those rates had proved just and proper at that time, particularly as Europe was in a state of such total devastation that there was no yardstick as to how any given country would recover.

But for them to have truly reflected the value of each country's goods and services forever would have been a miracle. Individuals change continually. So do economies, but less predictably, for it is always impossible to predict future government interference in the supply-demand equation.

Government Methods

Governments historically find themselves unable to resist offering their electorates greater and greater "benefits" (taking blood from the left arm and giving it to the right, losing 50% between the two) in an effort to stay in power. But in order to carry out these promises, even partially, they have had to get a lot of money from somewhere. They have taxed part of it from the rich to give to the poor, but it has not been possible to get enough in this way and so governments have been forced to borrow. There is a distinct limit to the amount they have been able to borrow genuinely from private individuals who wish to save and who trust the government with their savings. In fact this source seems now to be drying up on them. This is proven by the record rates government must offer to attract buyers for government paper.

As confidence in government has waned the price of bonds has collapsed, thus forcing up the rates of interest payable on them. Governments *can* dictate the amount they want to borrow but if they do so they give up all control over interest rates. And for both political and economic reasons it makes no sense to force interest rates into the sky.

They have been unable to tax enough or borrow enough from genuine savings and so they have had to resort increasingly to inflation. Governments have borrowed from the banks, who have used the resulting government bonds as collateral against which to increase their reserves. These measures have been undertaken in part pursuance of the welfare mirage "everything for everyone" and of the neo-Keynesian theories of artificially keeping the economy "buoyant." The moment there seems to be a downturn on the way, unsoundly financed government expenditure is undertaken to try to alleviate the situation. Unfortunately, however, the second prerequisite of deficit financing is conveniently forgotten. In the ensuing upturn the money created during the depression is never repaid or recouped. The money supply rises constantly (in Great Britain, for example, it rose 9.9% in 1968) and if you increase the money supply, prices must rise.

Inflation and Velocity

It may be fashionable to say here, "Ah yes, but not if the velocity of circulation is reduced," and this may be theoretically true but the pressures of inflation *increase* velocity rather than reduce it. Velocity rate is currently back to its extreme rate not seen since 1929. The private sector sees the value of money falling so it will not increase savings and will not invest unless interest rates or potential capital gains or tax benefits are huge. It tends to spend now in case prices are higher next year.

The faster the rate of inflation the faster will be the velocity of circulation as witnessed in 1920's hyper-inflation in Germany. Monetary circulation only increases after inflation has set in; it will not start by itself. Indeed it can only increase indefinitely if inflation is rife because under normal circumstances, i.e. no inflation, the fluctuation is merely seasonal.

Government action to alleviate the position of the dollar has tended to have entirely the wrong effect, simply because governments do not appear to understand what is causing the trouble. They are not villains, but sophisticated ignorance can create as much havoc as evil intentions. Governments seem to look on investors, speculators and dealers of any sort as the big bad wolves who are just waiting to plunge the whole world into chaos so they can benefit, instead of honest men trying to protect their property against government mismanagement.

Cold Comfort?

Nor is there any comfort in the US gold hoard. The truth is that America has no gold she can call her own. All her monetary backing is technically the property of her debtors. However, because of mirror tricks the gold sits in the USA and is counted as wholly owned assets.

Inflation Rate

Recently the inflation rate in the US has been running at approximately 6% which is twice what is considered acceptable or "safe." As stated earlier, either enforced deflation and devaluation *or* no-control inflation appears to be the alternative when inflation reaches this level.

The Rt. Hon. Hugh Gaitskell when British Chancellor of the Exchequer in 1951 made what looks now like a profound prophetic statement: "I must draw the attention of the Committee and of the country to a real danger which, because we in this country have in the past successfully avoided it, is often ignored; the danger that, if incomes and prices rise swiftly and continuously, there may be a progressive loss of confidence in the value of money. Were such confidence to be lost we should be plunged into inflation of the most violent kind, which in other countries has on more than one occasion brought the whole fabric of their social and political life to the edge of disaster."

This now appears to be happening. Until recently, it has

HOW AMERICA'S "FORGOTTEN MEN" HAVE CONTRIBUTED TO THE "SUCCESS" OF INFLATION

(billions of dollars)

YEAR	Private life ins. & pension reserves	Govt. Soc. Security & pension reserves	Savings deposits in all banks	Sav. & In. deposits, Cr. Unions, & postal savings	Savings in cash & idle bank accounts	U.S. Govt. secs. held by indivs.	State munic., & corporate bonds held by indivs.	Mortgages held by individuals	TOTAL	Relative purch'g power of dollar*	Annual percent deprec. of dollar	Annual loss of purch'g power
1940	29.7	7.4	26.5	5.8	13.3	10.6	29.9	12.0	135.2	99.0	1.0	1.4
41	31.9	9.3	26.6	6.5	14.9	13.6	29.0	12.2	144.0	90.2	8.9	12.8
42	34.4	11.8	27.1	6.7*	21.5	23.7	29.7	12.2	167.1	82.7	8.3	13.9
43	37.7	15.7	31.1	7.7	32.7	37.6	28.1	11.6	202.2	80.1	3.1	6.3
44	41.8	20.7	37.6	9.1	43.1	53.3	26.1	11.3	243.0	78.4	2.1	5.1
45	46.7	25.8	45.6	10.8	53.2	64.1	25.6	12.1	283.9	76.7	2.2	6.2
46	50.5	29.4	50.8	12.4	48.7	64.2	24.6	13.1	293.7	64.9	15.4	45.2
47	54.4	32.9	53.0	13.8	45.2	65.6	24.2	14.6	303.7	59.5	8.3	25.2
48	58.5	36.4	54.5	15.0	41.8	65.5	25.7	15.8	313.2	57.9	2.7	8.5
49	62.9	38.8	55.6	16.5	43.1	66.3	26.2	16.7	326.1	59.1	+2.1	+6.8
1950	68.1	41.4	56.3	17.9	37.6	66.3	28.2	17.8	333.6	55.8	5.6	18.7
51	73.5	44.1	59.0	20.0	39.5	64.6	30.2	19.4	350.3	52.7	5.6	19.6
52	80.0	48.5	63.6	23.1	38.8	65.1	33.0	20.6	372.7	52.3	0.8	3.0
53	86.8	51.8	68.4	26.9	39.5	64.9	36.4	21.8	396.5	51.9	0.8	3.2
54	98.0	54.3	73.5	31.6	37.4	63.5	37.9	23.4	419.6	52.1	+0.4	+1.7
55	100.0	57.4	76.8	36.6	30.0	64.7	42.2	25.4	433.1	52.0	0.2	0.9
56	107.0	61.1	80.9	41.8	25.0	65.5	42.3	27.3	450.9	50.5	2.9	13.1
57	114.2	64.3	88.1	46.7	21.3	64.9	45.7	29.3	474.5	49.0	3.0	14.2
58	124.7	64.9	97.5	53.0	19.9	63.7	46.8	32.5	503.0	48.2	1.6	8.0
59	133.8	67.2	101.1	60.0	13.1	69.4	47.5	35.4	527.5	47.5	1.5	7.9
1960	143.4	70.6	119.6	77.2	10.5	66.1	50.2	38.0	575.6	46.8	1.5	8.6
61	156.8	71.7	120.8	88.5	8.8	65.9	51.7	41.9	606.1	46.5	0.6	3.6
62	164.0	74.7	139.2	100.8	6.4	66.1	52.5	44.0	647.7	45.9	1.3	8.4
63	178.2	79.0	155.3	115.7	0.9	68.2	54.4	45.9	697.6	45.2	1.7	11.9
64	193.7	84.4	175.8	128.8	1.0	69.7	57.7	47.7	758.8	44.7	1.1	8.3
65	209.3	89.7	199.4	140.1	1.5	72.1	59.6	48.7	820.4	43.8	2.0	16.4
66	214.9	95.9	213.8	145.5	2.0	74.7	63.6	50.4	860.8	42.4	3.2	27.5
67	236.0	107.2	242.7	156.2	1.9	74.1	66.8	52.1	937.0	41.1	3.0	28.1
68e	250.0	115.5	268.0	165.0	2.5	76.3	69.8	54.0	1001.1	39.3	4.3	43.0

occurred so slowly that the loss in purchasing power has been barely noticed. However, the inflation chart (p.70) shows that it has indeed taken place and is escalating. Also the cumulative effect is now being felt. A World War I widow, for example, with her pension and fixed interest bonds, has become a welfare case because of it.

Inflation today is probably a lot higher than *admitted* inflation, for not only does government "seasonally adjust" all figures, but the whole system is so complex that it is merely a question of what you *call* inflation, of how much credit and non-money-money increase you include. The cost of services is not properly evaluated in Commerce Department figures—and it represents the *biggest* area of inflation. In the final essence, every mortgage or rental agreement is inflation, for it is buying goods with money that at the time doesn't exist; thus at that moment you personally have increased the money supply. Hopefully you reduce that supply as you make payments over a period of time with actual money. But the increases still outweigh the reduction of debt, on balance. Government is doing the same thing on an even bigger scale. The *true* inflation rate is, I believe, always the same as the common interest rate you can earn on money, well secured. In 1969 this would mean an inflation rate between 6 and 8%.

Hence all things considered, it looks as if it is time to look for other havens for repositories and investment, time to consider the VALUE as well as the numerical count of your capital; so in our next chapter we'll deal with the question: where?

	Retail Price Indices 1914–65		*1958 = 100*	
	Britain	United States	France	Germany
1914	24	35	0.56	43
1915	29	35	—	—
1916	34	38	—	—
1917	41	45	—	—
1918	47	54	—	—
1919	51	62	1.34	—
1920	58	69	1.90	456
1921	53	62	1.72	536
1922	43	58	1.68	2,310
1923	41	59	1.87	1,613,345
1924	41	59	2.06	54
1925	41	60	2.18	61
1926	40	61	2.71	61
1927	39	60	2.96	64
1928	39	59	2.90	66
1929	39	59	3.12	66
1930	37	57	3.28	63
1931	35	53	3.18	58
1932	34	47	2.96	51
1933	33	44	2.93	51
1934	33	46	2.90	52
1935	34	47	2.71	53
1936	35	48	2.84	53
1937	36	50	3.48	53
1938	37	49	3.93	54
1939	38	48	—	—
1940	43	48	—	—
1941	47	51	—	—
1942	50	56	—	—
1943	52	60	—	—
1944	53	61	—	—
1945	55	62	—	—
1946	57	68	—	—
1947	60	77	—	—
1948	64	83	49	85
1949	66	82	57	91
1950	68	83	63	85
1951	75	90	74	92
1952	81	92	83	94
1953	84	93	83	92
1954	85	93	82	92
1955	89	93	83	94
1956	94	94	85	96
1957	97	97	87	98
1958	100	100	100	100
1959	101	101	106	101
1960	102	102	110	102
1961	105	103	114	105
1962	110	105	119	108
	Britain	United States	France	Germany
1963	112	106	125	111
1964	115	107	130	114
1965	121	109	132	118

Note: The two breaks in the German figures, in 1924 and 1948, indicate introduction of a new monetary unit.

Sources: **League of Nations** *Statistical Yearbooks. International Financial Statistics. Historical Statistics of the U.S.A.; Key Statistics 1900–64* (London and Cambridge Economic Service).

PART 2

*Foreign Havens
(the "Where" Factor)*

CHAPTER 5

Where to Look

"Patriotism is your conviction that your country is superior to all others because you were born in it." George Bernard Shaw

ONCE the decision has been made that some part of one's assets *should* be moved, then one starts a search for the place to put them.

As nothing is certain, and as relatively few people want physically to leave their country of origin just because the money seems to be becoming unstable, then we are obviously only talking about the moving of a portion of one's assets. Initially this portion may be quite small (i.e. 10% of total assets or less) and then you can always add to it if you find foreign investing profitable or if things get worse on the home front.

It may also be that once you get used to the idea of international investment, you will start to think in terms of international markets in regard to your own business, in which case it will become necessary to have more money abroad, to cover the mechanics of international trading. But that is the future. In this chapter we are merely concerned with making the first move.

Reasons for Looking

Some of the things looked for are obvious. If you have decided to move some money because certain economic things are wrong in your own country, then it is logical that you would look for lack of those failures in the new country for investment.

There is another, secondary, reason for investing

abroad, which applies during *all* segments of the monetary cycle, and that is rate of growth.

America in the civilization and industrialization cycle has reached a slowing-down. This isn't referring to anything connected with a depression, but simply to the law of diminishing returns. In the early stages of a country's history the growth rate is fast, but as it becomes older, more civilized and more prosperous, the growth rate tends to level off. This means that more and more stocks become of the "blue chip" class, which makes them relatively nondynamic.

Recently in Australia, for example, the mining shares have been very attractive to the foreign buyer. The mining boom in Australia closely resembled the California gold rush of the last century. This is because Australia is much more of a pioneer country and so has much more by way of untapped wealth which once discovered moves into exciting boom conditions quite fast. However, this sort of speculation almost needs a prospecting mentality in the buyer as well, and the willingness to take a gamble for the potential of big profits. It is possible that similar situations will arise in the future in various parts of Africa, or even in the Amazon Basin (although in this area one has a currency depreciation problem to cope with on all investments). Japan is another strong growth rate area. But the point is that investing in a fast-growing country can be a fine bonus factor in your investment policy.

If you are primarily moving money as an "insurance policy" against possible loss at home, then the following points must be looked for in the country you finally settle on as a "haven in a storm."

Stock market performance around the world						
COUNTRY	INDEX	LATEST CLOSE Dec. 22, 1969	MONTH AGO Nov. 21, 1969	% CHANGE Since Nov. 20, 1969	YEAR AGO Dec. 20, 1968	% CHANGE Since Year Ago
AUSTRALIA	Sydney Ordinary	614.89	604.41	+ 1.7	584.22	+ 5.2
CANADA	Toronto Industrials	183.31	184.65	— 0.7	188.13	— 2.6
FRANCE	INSII	132.5	131.1	+ 1.1	104.9	+ 26.3
GERMANY	Herstatt	128.66	134.78	— 4.5	115.70	+ 11.2
HOLLAND	Amsterdam Industrials	122.0	125.2	— 2.6	398.8	+ 5.5
ITALY	24 Ore-Il Sole	70.42	74.47	— 5.4	62.48	+ 12.7
JAPAN	DJIA	2258.26	2201.52	+ 2.6	1702.45	+ 32.6
SWITZERLAND	Swiss Bank Corp.	335.9	343.9	— 2.3	326.8	+ 2.8
U.K.	Financial Times	394.1	389.8	+ 1.1	495.7	— 20.5
USA	DJIA	785.97	823.13	— 4.5	966.99	— 18.7

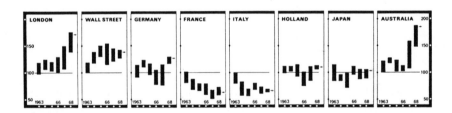

These charts taken at random are typical of many over recent years (especially since 1966) which show that there is money to be made in some stock market somewhere in the world most of the time. It also may be revealing to those Americans who don't realize many other markets have been doing much better than US markets.

1. Stability of the currency

This can be checked by looking at its record for the last 50 years or so to see how many times the country in question has devalued, and for what reasons. If it has merely devalued with others at times of *world* financial crisis, then the currency is probably as stable as any you will find, but if it has an exceptional history of frequent devaluation then to put your assets in a bank account in such a country would in most cases be foolish. Two examples of what I mean are France and Germany. In recent years, both countries have had much more stable money than in their pasts. But both have proved that there is something in the social structure which means it could happen again. However, in the case of Germany there ARE a number of attractive investment opportunities. So in such cases, the wise course is to open your bank account in a more stable haven, and then to invest through that haven in other countries.

2. A history of neutrality

It is always embarrassing to find that some haven you have chosen for your money suddenly becomes an enemy of your country, or even gets involved in a war elsewhere. There are very few countries that have a long history of neutrality, in Europe only Switzerland and Sweden. Neutrality is not a banking must, but it's a strong plus factor.

3. Banking privacy

It is not that you want to do any thing illegal, but to have an account abroad that any ex-wife, or would-be bringer of a lawsuit, or a man idly checking your net worth, etc. could call up and get information on would not be exactly desirable. Also, if banking privacy is the code of behavior, then it usually means privacy even from the local government, and this is an indication of a totally free country. It is also a measure of banking integrity,

4. Lack of government intervention

This again is a yardstick of freedom.

5. A democratic country, with political stability

Any country under a dictatorship automatically has state-controlled money, and the value can change at the drop of a hat—his hat! This means that although the currency might be stable today, it could become weak very fast. A recent example of this is France. Although France is technically a democracy, under de Gaulle it became a sort of benevolent dictatorship. While this stabilized the franc in a way that it had almost never been stabilized in the past, it did mean that it created a climate which made it possible for the franc to go from being *very* strong to *very* weak, more or less overnight. No doubt many foreigners who had put their money into France on the basis of de Gaulle's "new look" franc lost very heavily when the parity rate suddenly broke, well before France devalued, because there was no warning of disaster.

6. Conservative banking laws

It is well to look into the banking laws of the country you are considering. If the banking laws are lax, if it is easy to open and operate a bank, if the issuance of credit against deposits isn't tightly controlled then the bank could overextend itself (just as a man on too much margin) and get into difficulty if judgment is merely a shade off.

7. A sound backing for the currency

By this is meant, how much gold is there in the public treasury? An example of a really sound currency is the Swiss franc, which is backed by gold, varying from 85% to 135%.

8. Internationally recognized status as a money center

This shows itself when for example you are stranded in the middle of the Congo and run out of money. What check can be cashed at a local bank? Or at any rate, what check can you get cashed the fastest?

9. The reciprocal laws between the country in question and your own

What your new banking country tells your old banking country at *this* stage may not matter. But should the worst happen, as for example in Germany during World War II, then lack of reciprocal information would be an asset. As a Jew or out-of-favor citizen in Germany in World War II you would certainly have been grateful for such privacy. You can think of other examples, I daresay, in many countries.

10. Freedom of movement for currency

In other words no exchange control, or at any rate, no exchange control that affects you as an alien. It is, however, always well to examine the exchange control laws very carefully, whether they effect you or not, for they may indicate a trend and point to total restriction of the currency in the future. This is essential, for while your chosen haven may look perfect now there is always a chance that it will change, especially if it has been moving in the direction of restriction.

11. *The national characteristics of the people*

If a people have what might loosely be called "flair," such as the Italians and the South Americans, then the chances are that as bankers they are less than stable. It takes a certain "dullness," if you like, of personality to make a good banker: caring about the money first and the human element second. You need a banker who is a stickler for detail, who is slow to "make deals" or to negotiate, or to compromise himself. Also, a country *with* flair or artistic emotion often tends towards riots and national hysteria in one form or another. This element can trigger a local financial crisis with a depreciation of currency the result.

How to Check

When checking out various countries, if you write to the commerce departments, the boards of trade, and foreign branches of American banks they will usually send you information of the banking facilities for foreigners in that country. This will also give you an indication as to how much English is spoken there, for unless you speak the local language the ability to communicate with your foreign bank in English is obviously of the utmost importance.

The local tax laws are of a certain interest, and will be dealt with more fully in a later chapter; however, it is well to check out what will be deducted for local taxes on your interest and capital gains, and also if there is a reciprocal tax agreement with the USA whereby you can claim one against the other. If taxes are high, and no such agreement exists, you could find yourself paying high local taxes, and then having to pay full US taxes as well. Either the banks or the tax office in the countries concerned will supply

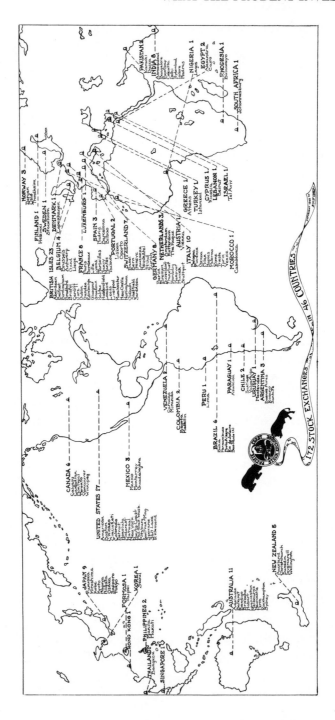

basic information on this, and of course your tax man in the US can usually look up to see where such agreements exist.

Having checked out the points listed in this chapter you are then ready to move on to other considerations, such as investment opportunities. So we shall now explore specific countries to see what they have to offer.

CHAPTER 6

Specific Havens

"If you destroy a free market you create a black market. If you have ten thousand regulations you destroy all respect for the law." Winston Churchill

FOR the ordinary international investor there are relatively few countries where there is any practical possibility of investment. Of course the *professional* speculator on an international level can go in and out of some special situation (like a mine) in a remote or minor country, but for most of us, investing in countries that we are somewhat familiar with, and which are relatively stable, seems to be more practical for our activity abroad.

While I propose to list various countries and their investment possibilities for Americans, I preface this with a list of the *methods* for investing in such places.

Methods for Investment Abroad

A few major foreign countries have stock brokerage representation in the USA, notably Canada and Japan, with offices in a number of large cities. The stock exchanges of every foreign country will supply you with the addresses of their American contacts, if such exist, through which you can buy their local shares. Apart from that the easiest way to buy foreign investments is through a Swiss bank. The Swiss bank operates as a sort of *international* brokerage office and can obtain equities for you in any part of the world, if they are available to foreigners. It is also possible for you to obtain a list of local brokers in each country and trade *direct,* but this usually runs into all sorts of difficulties particularly in countries where the local language is not English.

Even where English is spoken, such as in London, the procedure, information available, form of statements, etc. are so different from anything you have dealt with in the USA that the frustration involved, for some people, might not be worth the effort.

Japan

Because Japanese radios and electrical goods are sold so widely in the USA, many Americans in recent years have become keenly interested in Japanese stocks. The Japanese economy has had dynamic growth in the last decade, and names like Sony and Standard have become household words. Buying into any foreign market necessitates that you study the market concerned. The Japanese stock exchange was modeled very strongly on the US market. It even has a Dow Jones average of its own, denominated in Yen, to enable you to chart the trend. You should be aware that some of their share price/earnings ratios are often as high as in the US. Major cities in the USA have Japanese brokerage offices, which will supply information and views on the Japanese market. The largest Japanese brokers operating within the USA are Nikko Securities, Nomura Securities, Yamaichi Securities, and Daiwa Securities. These four are all to be found in both New York City and London. Nomura claims to be the second largest securities dealer in the world after Merrill Lynch.

Australia

The Australian investment scene has been of great interest in recent times, owing largely to the fact that it tends to be as America *was*. In other words, Australia in many ways is still a pioneering country, so when something starts to move, the growth curve is dynamic. Also, there

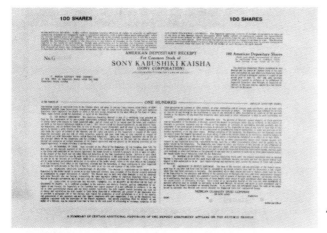

ADR of Sony

Share Certificate of
Yawata Iron & Steel

Share Certificate
of Toshiba

has recently been a lot of mining activity which is akin to the California gold rush, although on an infinitely larger scale. This type of growth potential always interests the American. However, as with any fast growth item the risk element is also quite high.

South Africa (& ADR's)

The main interest here, to outsiders, has been the gold mining shares and mining finance companies. However, the industrial side of South Africa should not be ignored, for it has been one of the biggest gainers among world exchanges in recent years. Because of exchange control and unique procedures, most people buy South African shares through a Swiss bank or a London broker or banker, the Swiss bank being the easier way. But there are certain South African shares, and indeed a smattering of foreign stocks around the world that have an "ADR" (American Depository Receipt) on them. This means that they have once been bought by an American, and he paid the interest equalization tax on them, and now they are traded as American shares, theoretically at a higher price which allows for the tax. This is often the easiest way for an American to buy foreign shares, if he can find the shares he wants with ADR's. If he buys non-ADR foreign shares through an American brokerage house, and most of the bigger houses will buy and sell a few foreign issues, then the brokerage house is bound by law to file an IRS form on his behalf showing that the share has been bought for his account. With ADR's this is not so, for they are treated as US shares for tax purposes.

Canada

Probably this is the easiest foreign market for the US citizen and several major US cities have Canadian brokerage houses. Also, many American brokers will buy

Canadian issues for you, and some have Canadian associates. The beauty of Canada is that statistically the market is similar to that of the United States. Most other foreign markets supply very little by way of statistics, which is very frustrating to an American. Also, the market is big enough for there to be a ready market to sell and buy the listed shares. The main interest for Americans in Canada tends to be their mining shares, but certainly not exclusively so.

Europe

Europe like Japan is an industrial area, so investment interest throughout Europe is primarily industry shares. There are many European companies that are well known names in the USA, including Germany's Grundig and Volkswagen, or Italy's Olivetti. Trading Euro issues necessitates following the individual European markets and their political movements quite closely to enable the foreigner to invest intelligently, unless of course he does it on the advice of an international banker or broker, or a Swiss banker who is both. Despite the effort required, there are from time to time a number of worthy opportunities for investment. There are also opportunities to lend money to other countries, notably European, denominated in Swiss francs and repayable in Swiss francs. Other currency denominations are available but none safer or stronger and thus I personally don't recommend them during the current period of monetary nervousness. However, all other currencies pay higher yields. You get what you pay for in both interest and peace of mind, in all investments.

Switzerland

Although Switzerland is part of Europe, it has certain peculiarities which are its own. For example the Zurich stock exchange lists a number of American issues, a little over three dozen, and it is possible to buy them there as easily as in the US. There are also a number of Swiss issues, ranging from chocolate manufacturers like Nestle and Suchard to big pharmaceutical and chemical firms. One can also actually buy shares in the Swiss banks themselves. Hence Switzerland is both a national and an international brokerage. You can buy local shares or, through its banks, buy shares from anywhere in the world. But the facilities of Swiss banks are reserved for the next chapter.

Exchange Control

Of the countries mentioned above only Canada and Switzerland are completely free from any sort of exchange control. These are the restrictions which prevent local inhabitants from taking unlimited funds out of their country. In some nations the exchange control laws also apply to foreigners, which means that if you take money into a country to start up a business or buy stock you will have an awkward time getting capital and/or profits out. It is therefore necessary before investing in any foreign country personally (i.e. direct, not through a Swiss bank) to check out the exchange control laws fully. England has rigid controls whereas most of Europe has only mild ones. French controls have changed frequently of late.

Of course investment through a Swiss bank insulates against exchange controls because the Swiss cover themselves, and are conversant with local laws. But it is a necessary piece of research if you intend to invest *direct*.

How Tied to Pound Sterling and US Dollar

Australia and South Africa are pretty well tied to the pound sterling. This doesn't mean that they are backed by the pound. It means that because they trade so much with England the chances are that their currency may follow in any pound sterling devaluation, even if by a smaller percentage. However, in the case of South Africa a gold investment, while denominated in Rands, is a counter-devaluation hedge.

Japan and Canada are tied very closely to the US dollar and should the dollar get into real trouble they would likely be badly hit by its backwash. In these two cases, not only are they big trading partners of the US but their treasuries hold a great many dollars.

The reason of course why a country that is closely linked by trade to another is forced to devalue when the trading partner does is a question of competition. Once the trading partner has devalued, suddenly the other side can't stand the competition of the cheaper prices of the competitor and they too often have to devalue as a sort of retaliatory measure. Revaluing works the same in reverse (i.e., upvaluing).

Conclusion

While it is possible to invest *direct* in most countries, and in some ways it is an advantage to do so (if you go through Switzerland you often have to pay double commission, the Swiss commission plus the brokerage commission in the country into which you are buying), it isn't always wisest. Both for the sophisticated and for the uninitiated, the Swiss banker acts as a sort of insulation against the problems of "going foreign" and is therefore usually worth the extra cost. If time is money then the time you save by letting your Swiss banker handle the details is greater than his commission.

CHAPTER 7

Foreign Investments Other Than Stocks and Bonds

"Every time History repeats itself the price goes up." Anon.

ONCE you start thinking in terms of investing on an international basis, all sorts of investments other than stocks and bonds become available. Some of the things mentioned below can technically be done in the USA, but usually the mechanics are so complicated and the people able to perform the service so unwilling as to make it impossible in real terms.

Gold

Gold bars (of various sizes) can be purchased with comparative ease by almost anyone in most of continental Europe, Canada, Mexico, the Middle East, and a few other assorted places. It's normally done through banks. In most cases the bank does not inquire about the buyer's nationality. Thus many Americans have reportedly bought gold. However, a presidential proclamation has declared it is illegal for an American citizen to own gold "either directly or indirectly." That means that not only must a US citizen not own bullion, but he cannot own any form of gold-backed bond or paper, or fund that has gold as part of its portfolio. He cannot own gold coins either, except those prior to 1933, and only in amounts that would classify them as collector's items. This is an area where the foreign bank will not be your conscience; you must be your own.

Silver

Silver can most easily be bought through London, or through a Swiss bank, which usually buys it for you in

London. Its form is the same as in the US, that is you can either buy bullion outright or else buy a contract (a "future") on margin. If you take delivery on the bullion, the bank will of course charge you a small storage fee. The reason people buy silver contracts in London is that not only do they have a speculation in silver, but it is a short against the pound at the same time, for they are substituting silver for the second currency, as explained later in the section on shorting currencies. Your silver contract, in London, is written in pounds no matter what currency you pay in.

There is also a constant threat, or possibility, that the US government will close the American futures market in silver. In this case those holding futures would lose their position, and might lose money (depending on purchase price). If one buys silver through a Swiss bank, most banks will allow you then to use the bullion as a security to cover other investments, which gives a degree of leverage to your investment capital not normally possible elsewhere. The percentage of loan value will vary between banks and even between *customers*, but is usually in the region of enabling you to borrow 80% against gold and 70% against silver

Swiss Gold Markets

No book on Switzerland would be complete without at least a reference to its gold market, even though it isn't likely to affect you. Your interest is therefore mainly academic. The two biggest gold markets in the world are London and Zurich. In 1969 there was keen competition between the two. In early 1970 the edge seems to have gone back to London, but this is greatly disputed by some Swiss who say they do more volume than London by far, but it's not reported; it's between banks. Hard facts are illusive on volume.

Zurich sells gold bullion (in a variety of size bars) and gold futures and gold coin. Zurich is not exclusive in this respect. Any Swiss city can accommodate you, but things tend to focalize on Zurich for gold.

In Switzerland you can get gold for currency or currency for gold, the ultimate in convertibility. This is perfection in monetary safety and in protection of individual liberty. One can only hope that more countries will move toward full convertibility.

Gold futures work rather like commodity or currency futures; they are simply a forward contract to buy bullion at a price fixed in time, for a fee. Their popularity ebbs and flows largely with credit conditions.

Gold shares are also easily available in Switzerland. Several South African gold shares are actually listed on the Zurich stock exchange, so the commission is minimal. My research indicates a large percentage of portfolios which are domiciled in Switzerland probably have gold shares in them.

The quality of gold share research varies widely in Switzerland, from nil to highly exemplary. Unfortunately Switzerland is a backward, underdeveloped nation in the area of stock *charts,* so that gold shares (and any other shares) do not get much technical knowledge backing them up. Swiss bankers (with a few notable exceptions) tend to give advice on fundamentals, not because they don't believe in charts and technical factors so much as that they don't understand chart reading. They often cover up this lack of chart knowledge by claiming they don't believe in its merits. But I think it's fair to say that generally no one can discard or disparage a tool or field of knowledge until he understands it and tests it. So, in gold shares and every other share and every other kind of market, the Swiss are, on the whole, fundamentalists, not chartists. Ideally one should be both.

Diamonds and Other Precious Stones

This is a very specialized form of investment, and is not advised unless you have some prior knowledge of gems. If however you do have a knowledge and wish to own precious stones as an investment, then they can be bought through a merchant in Europe and stored in a safe deposit box, preferably in a Swiss bank. You can also make arrangements with a Swiss bank for it to get an art or diamond appraiser to work on your behalf.

Shorting and Buying Other Currencies

Possibly the thing which most quickly conjures up pictures of the big operator and/or those "gnomes of Zurich" is stories of the currency speculators bringing down a currency.

But what exactly *is* buying a currency forward or selling it short? Is it just too remote from your everyday life for you to bother with? Not really. Anybody who trades commercially on an international basis, buys or shorts a currency at some time or another.

For example: an Englishman wishing to buy wheat from Canada may transact the deal in Canadian dollars. As the pound *has* been devalued relatively recently and the Canadian dollar *hasn't*, this particular Englishman *may* feel that the Canadian dollar is not as stable a currency as the pound. There will be a time lag, owing to ocean shipment, harvesting, etc., before he actually *receives* the wheat. If he can hold off payment for as long as possible then it could be to his advantage for he might get "cheaper" Canadian dollars for his pounds if a devaluation has occurred.

The Canadian farmer, on the other hand, feeling doubtful about his own currency and having failed to make the deal in pounds, will cover the time lag between shipment of the wheat and the payment by selling Canadian dollars short. If the C-dollar is devalued, then although he will get less VALUE in *payment*, he will make up the difference on his short sale profit. He may in fact make an extra profit, depending on the percentage of devaluation and the timing.

If the Canadian, still believing that the dollar might go down before the pound, had been buying some item *from* England in pounds he could have done one of the following to cover the transaction:

1. Sell his Canadian dollars *short*, as mentioned above, against the pound.

2. Buy his pounds *now*, on the assumption that he would have to pay more dollars for them later. He would pay the "spot" rate.

3. Buy pounds *forward*. That is, agree to take delivery on the fixed number of pounds in the future at a pre-determined rate. Naturally he pays a premium for this.

4. He can settle the invoice in advance.

This isn't pure speculation. It is merely the trader's way of fixing a currency rate, so that when he and a foreign trader make a bargain, the currency rate will (within their bargain) be the same at the end of the transaction as it was when they first negotiated . . . at least for them.

Now enters that "terrible speculator" you read about in the press. Politicians berate him, yet he provides vital market stability. The mechanics of what he does are exactly the same as the international trader's. The only difference is that his motives for doing it are merely that he feels a currency is likely to be devalued or revalued, and he hopes he will be able to make a profit (often 100%) on his ability to see the trend in currencies. If he feels a currency is weak, then he chooses a currency that is strong against which to short it. The mechanics he uses are very similar to the commodity market's, except in place of the commodity he uses a second currency.

The entire transaction of currency buying, selling and shorting can be done with almost any Swiss bank, a number of London and Continental banks, and a few American banks. But as most American banks are unsophisticated in this area, and as London has an exchange control problem, clearly your best bet is a Swiss bank.

You do not have to cover the full cost of the transaction. It is like commodities where you put up only a small percentage of the value of the contract. However, when trading in currencies, the "margin cost" on each currency varies (i.e. the interest rate). When you trade on margin with your brokerage house the cost of borrowing the money for margin is always the same whereas with currencies the interest rate varies according to currency. For example if it costs you, say, 8% to borrow a particular currency for a year, and the amount you expect a devaluation to be is, say, 10%, then it becomes only marginally profitable (i.e. 2.8% return) to speculate in the currency, *if* it takes a full year for the devaluation to occur. If it takes over a year you will lose money. Ideally you should buy or sell short a currency only a few weeks before its parity is altered. If you do so you can make 75-100% profit, due to margin. Otherwise interest eats up your small margin on a contract.

The most conservative way to speculate in currencies of course is to keep your money *in* a strong currency and *out* of a weak one, transferring cash assets from one to another from time to time as situations change. This way you avoid interest charges, and can sit in, say, Deutschmarks, or Swiss francs and get interest on the account as well. Usually the interest rates paid on a strong currency are less than on a weak one, but that is the price of safety.

One place in the USA which gladly handles currency futures is the newly functioning International Commercial Exchange, 2 Broadway, New York, New York 10004. This is conveniently close for Americans but requires a higher margin than Switzerland. Also see the list of banks listed later in the book.

Your *local* US banker, however, is likely to regard you as a visitor from Mars if you asked him to buy a forward contract for you in, say, Japanese Yen.

Eurodollars

This is another term that one hears a lot of, and yet which sounds far too sophisticated for the average investor. However, the concept again is very simple.

Eurodollars are defined technically as dollar assets held by banks or people *outside* the US, regardless of whether these assets are owned by US residents or not. These funds are used, in the main, for lending operations, for short, medium and long-term financing. The Eurodollar market is thus mainly made up of banks which accept deposits on dollar accounts and use these for dollar loans not only to other banks but also to companies and institutions.

The name Eurodollar is technically incorrect, as the market is limited neither to Europe nor to dollar transactions. Canadian and Japanese and Singapore banks also operate in the Eurodollar market and transactions are carried out in a number of currencies such as Swiss francs, D-marks, etc. In fact any currency deposited in a bank outside the country in which it is legal tender can be part of the Eurodollar market. However, four-fifths of the market is actually conducted in US dollars.

London is the center of the Eurodollar market, and dominates it.

The private American citizen participates in this market by having an account in a foreign bank (usually Swiss but sometimes English) and then lending out his money on Eurodollar loans, which are deposits lent for a fixed period of time at a fixed rate of interest. Currently the Eurodollar rates are the highest of any form of "time deposits" available. However, the rates fluctuate considerably and so should be watched carefully, for timing your arrangements.

Trust Agreements

If you deposit dollars in Switzerland and they earn interest, then the Swiss tax authorities deduct 30% tax at source. The bank has to deduct this on behalf of the tax authorities. However, it is possible to set up a situation called a trust agreement, whereby the Swiss bank is not legally the place where you have deposited money but merely acts as your agent. This means that instead of depositing your money with the bank, having the bank guarantee it, and then on its own risk using the money to earn interest, part of which you receive as deposit interest, the bank merely places your dollars entirely at your risk in a third country in some form of interest-bearing investment. The money placed abroad on your behalf is placed in the bank's name so anonymity is safeguarded. Under this agreement the 30% Swiss tax is not payable. The risk in practice involved is very small because most of this money is put into London's giant banks. If you pay the 30% tax it means that if you earn 3% on your money you only receive 2% net, on 4% you net 2.8%, on 5% you net

3.5%, on 6% you net 4.2%. If you adopt the trust agreement arrangement, for a slight risk you gain considerably.
These agreements are gaining in popularity.

Time Deposits

This is simply money on deposit with a bank, for which
you get paid a higher rate of interest than for a normal
deposit account, in return for leaving a given sum of
money for a fixed amount of time. They are a cousin to a
certificate of deposit. Most Swiss banks have some kind of
time deposit though they go under a wide variety of
names. They also vary from 3 months to 12 months, and
can be in US dollars or Swiss francs.

Other "International Paper"

It is said that most Arabs don't buy stocks and shares.
Talk to a Swiss banker and the chances are he will admit
that Arabs (with the exception of the newly converted)
feel there are only two forms of investment, gold and
interest rates. In other words, they make their investment
money not by buying stocks with a possibility of capital
gain, but by moving money in and out of various countries
depending on interest rates. They balance rates against
stability of currency, and hope to switch over before a
currency falls. Perhaps we have something to learn from
them, for there must be a significance in what people do
with their money who have to live in one of the most
politically unstable areas of the world. This is a region
where millionaires and rulers are being deposed, exiled,
etc. almost daily, and so it is vital in any Arab's investment
plan that he be covered if he loses everything he has at
home.

The various types of "paper" are too numerous and/or
specialized to list, but basically they all work the same:
You lend a sum of money to a person, people, corporation,

government, etc. in a particular currency for a set period at a fixed rate of interest. The longer the period the higher the interest (usually) because the risk is greater. A good Swiss banker can discuss the ramifications of the various sorts of paper with you. Some banks offer specialized paper. One has a 364-day Certificate of Deposit, which avoids the US Interest Equalization tax and pays a substantial interest. Again, a good Swiss banker can discuss these types of paper with you. Swiss CD's are also offered by Bank Leu & Cie in Zurich.

Funds Sold Abroad

There is a wide variety of non-US mutual funds throughout the world. They are rarely called mutual funds, except colloquially. In England they're called unit trusts. In Switzerland they are called investment trusts. Any Swiss bank will send you literature on them, as well as on funds in other countries.

There are many funds that specialize in Japanese stocks (either exclusively or partially) and these funds are not, oddly enough, found mostly in Japan, although there are some in Japan also (e.g. Japan Fund, which is listed on the New York Stock Exchange as well). A sampling of Japan-oriented funds may interest you. They include: Tokyo Trust SA (Panama-based, quoted on Luxembourg Stock Exchange and also sold through Nikko Securities), Nippon Fund (Bahamas-based), Japan Selection Fund (has Australian stocks also), Pacific Seaboard Fund (N.M. Rothschild, advisor), Jardine Japan Fund (managed by Jardine Matheson), Anglo-Nippon Trust, Robeco (internationally minded, Dutch-based), International Investment, Formula Selection, and Universal Trust.

Not only Swiss banks but almost any foreign bank will provide information about funds that are sold in their country.

The Swiss funds cater to almost every taste. They are few in number but offer considerable scope. They include: Europa-Valor (selected European stocks), Canasec (Canadian stocks), Intervalor (European and overseas shares), Japan Pacific Fund (Japanese and Pacific basin area stocks), Ussec (USA shares), Universal Fund (European and overseas shares), Energie-Valor (utility shares of various countries), Schweizeraktien (Swiss stocks), Swissvalor, Neue Serie (Swiss stocks), and there are at least eight real estate funds—all Swiss except one for Canada, and at least two mixed funds.

Summary: Where To Do This "Jet Set Investment"

In theory it is possible to pursue the sort of investment discussed in this chapter in any country in the world, but to deal directly with the countries concerned means that in order to invest, one's knowledge has to be equivalent to an international banker.

This of course is limiting. It means that if you are in Yen and have done your homework very thoroughly before investing in Japan, then when you want to move your money to say, Australia, you have to learn all about the Australian banking system, currency exchange rules, etc. The answer to this is to invest through a Swiss bank, for then the mechanics of local regulations are the headache and province of your banker. All you have to be concerned with is selecting the *type* of investment. Even this is simplified by asking for alternatives and then merely choosing from among them. Indeed Swiss bankers are seemingly born to deal in tangle and they thrive on a diet of details which are either baffling or boring to most of us.

PART 3

Swiss Banks
(the "Who" Factor)

CHAPTER 8

Swiss Bank Facilities

"The Swiss are indeed a hardworking people and this devotion to work is one of their most repulsive virtues." George Mikes

PERHAPS it is the hardworking and dedicated nature of the Swiss that makes Swiss banks the most comprehensive "investment shops" in the world. In the USA and indeed most other countries, your bank will provide some services, your stock broker others, and then when you want to deal in a foreign country you must go to that country to get the services you require. But the average Swiss bank is a "one stop" international investment house.

Facilities That Swiss Banks Can Offer You

1. They can simply "store" money for you, in complete safety. To many people who fear currency debasement in their country—or political problems—or whatever—this is justification enough. Switzerland's bank record for safety and longevity has no peer.
2. They can provide commercial "facilities" for business transactions anywhere in the world.
3. Offer higher (credit) margin for buying stock, etc. than most countries.
4. Give advice on worldwide investments (and especially European) with objectivity possible only through their neutral status, mid-Continent location, and centuries of investment precedent.
5. Actually make investment decisions for you, keep your capital working on your authority to let them act for your account and of course at your risk (i.e. operate for you under power of attorney).

6. Provide safekeeping facilities for everything from stock certificates to gold bars. However, because the Swiss value money, and husband it so well, it works both ways. That is, everything a Swiss bank will do for you, will cost you a fee, and usually the fee is slightly higher than you would pay in any other country for the same service.

7. Make you loans on quality Swiss or US stocks. Generally a more flexible loan is available (i.e. percent of value) than elsewhere.

8. Grant short and medium term credits to industry and commerce.

9. Provide overdraft facilities for selected private and corporate clients (i.e. you can overdraw your account and pay interest on the amount overdrawn).

10. Provide foreign exchange facilities in *all* currencies, not just the most popular ten.

11. Discounting of Swiss and foreign commercial acceptances up to 180 days (financing of accounts receivable).

12. They assist you in merchant-banking matters, such as mergers and acquisitions, corporate capital planning and reorganization, market-technical consulting, forming of holding companies, etc. Some banks will on occasion invest *with* you in a deal they arrange.

13. Funds kept in Switzerland in Swiss Francs are unfettered and have unrestricted utility and versatility.

14. Your Swiss banker's letter of introduction, given anywhere, carries more gravity, more weight than from elsewhere. He is more respected and letters are *not* casually given.

Types of Accounts Available

There is great variety within Switzerland, both in kinds of accounts and in rates paid, and it's always changing, but generally there are:

1. Swiss Franc "Deposit Accounts"—which pay deposi-

tors 3 to 4% interest at this time of writing.

2. US Dollar "Deposit Accounts." Often about 1% higher than the prevailing Swiss Franc rate. Range: from 0 to 6%, depending on money market conditions. Some pay 5% at time of writing.

3. Regular account, which pays no interest. Usually called a "current account."

4. Checking accounts in Swiss Francs. At a very few banks, interest is paid on checking accounts carrying a minimum balance.

5. Checking accounts in US dollars. At a very few banks, interest is paid on checking accounts carrying a minimum balance.

6. Investment accounts—which hold funds to invest in whatever securities are in keeping with policies of the bank and the general agreement of the client to either direct the bank or let the bank act on its own initiative via a power of attorney.

7. Trust Account Deposits. Starting from $25,000. Three- and six-month investments, paying the maximum international rates. Bank acts only as agent (see trust agreements, Chapter 7).

8. Fixed time deposits. Usually dollars and Swiss Franc amounts only. Will pay less than Eurodollar interest rate but tends to be in gear with it. Dollar accounts pay well above Swiss Franc accounts, since dollars are a higher risk currency.

In most cases foreign depositors have their money converted to Swiss Francs at the outset of their account. Often, however, accounts are kept in dollars, or both. Less frequently they are carried in other currencies. When one's currency is converted into Swiss Francs, it is done at the official rate for the day.

Many people have a variety of accounts, a deposit account, and checking account and an investment account.

The "Trading" Department of a Swiss Bank

Your Swiss bank will transact business for your account on all stock exchanges of the world. As it is not represented on exchanges outside Switzerland, it works with a network of correspondent banks and brokers with whom it has telex or telegraphic contact. The usual practice is to leave the purchased securities with the foreign correspondent bank for safekeeping, rather than with the broker. The bank selects its correspondents with Swiss care. Even so, you can request that securities be brought to your Swiss bank and kept there, without extra charge as a rule, or very little charge.

Stock exchange transactions on the US or Canadian exchanges can, like trading on any other market, be conducted through a Swiss bank. To do this costs the regular US or Canadian commission *plus* Swiss commission calculated as follows:

for *stocks:*

up to $40.00 per share: half of US or Canadian commission

$70.00 per share: five-eighths of US or Canadian commission

over $70.00 per share: three-quarters of US or Canadian commission

for *bonds:*

one-quarter percent of total cost (i.e. on $1000—$2.50)

for *T-Bills:*

$\frac{1}{8}\%$ for maturities 6 months and more

$1/16\%$ for maturities under 6 months

A number of US and Canadian shares are traded in Swiss Francs on Swiss exchanges. If these are bought in Switzerland then *only* the Swiss commission, ½% of total cost, is charged. In addition to such savings, another advantage of trading on the Swiss exchange is the short sale, which requires no "up-tick" before the trade is executed, unlike the New York exchange. Thus in a fast-falling market you can always get your short executed. This is a bear's paradise.

The U.S. stocks listed in Switzerland are as follows:

American Telephone & Telegraph

International Telephone and Telegraph

Burroughs Corporation
Caterpillar Tractor

Kennecott Copper
Kraftco (National Dairy Products)

Chesapeake & Ohio Railroad
Chrysler

Litton Industries
Louisiana Land & Expl. (listed only in Geneva)

Consolidated Natural Gas

Marcor (Montgomery Ward)

Continental Oil

Minnesota Mining and Manufacturing

CPC International (Corn Products)
Dow Chemical
E.I. Dupont de Nemours

Mobile Oil
National Cash Register
National Distillers and Chemical

Eastman Kodak
Ford Motors
General Electric
General Foods
General Motors
General Telephone and Electronics

Pacific Gas and Electric
Penn Central
Philip Morris
Procter & Gamble
Standard Oil of New Jersey

Union Carbide

Goodyear Tire   Uniroyal
I.B.M.   U.S. Steel
International Paper   Woolworth

There are a number of other foreign stocks traded on Swiss exchanges, among them are the two South African shares: Orange Free State Investment Trust and West Rand Investment Trust. Most Swiss banks will on request supply a list of foreign shares traded locally.

South African shares can be bought as South African registered (called "Cape delivery") or as London registered (London delivery). Speedier registration is the main advantage of London delivery, but beware of the "tax at source" of 26% British withholding tax which may be deducted on interest accruing on London delivery shares if the shares have not been registered in the name of a non-British holder. Conditions vary and change so you should get current advice at the time of trading on this.

Commissions on the London exchange are among the highest known. They are an all-inclusive 2¼% for the purchase and 1¼% for the sale. On top of this the Swiss commission of one-half the London commission is added for all shares bought by Switzerland for you from London.

Registration of Stocks

The Swiss bank buys stocks in its own name but for the account of its customer. For all outsiders *only* the name of the bank appears as the buyer or seller. In the case of registered shares (an Anglo-American practice) stocks will be registered in the name of the bank, or held in the street name by the correspondent. In the case of European stocks (frequently in bearer form) stocks are usually held with correspondent banks and will be stored in their vaults.

Swiss banks do not allow any customer to directly place an order with a broker for the account of his Swiss bank (sub-account himself). You can however deal directly with a broker abroad and pay with checks drawn on your Swiss account.

Buying Silver through a Swiss Bank

The minimum amount of silver that can be purchased through a Swiss bank is 5000 ounces and multiples thereof. The bank will store the silver for you for a fee, and charge you one-cent commission per ounce purchased ($50 on 5000 ounces). You can borrow money to buy silver bullion in Switzerland. Current arrangements are for a 25% margin. On what currency you wish to purchase the silver in, depends the interest charged. Currently, for example, if you borrow pound sterling, your interest rate on a silver bullion loan would be 12% per annum. If you wish to borrow US dollars the rate would be 11%, Swiss Francs 7%. Interest rates fluctuate from time to time, but the rate is usually set for six months and guaranteed for that period.

Swiss Companies

We can't leave you without a paragraph about Swiss corporations whose shares are listed. I shall not attempt a company-by-company analysis, but suffice it to say there are some Swiss corporate giants that are among the best managed firms in the world. They have almost no labor troubles, are not plagued by government restrictions (let alone ever *changing* government rules), and have a maximum of free market conditions in which to operate. Their profit records are excellent, by and large, and many a foreign investor has made sizable profits in recent years in such companies as Swissair and Suchard.

Perhaps the biggest advantage to Swiss corporate shares is the political stability in which they exist. Every country has *economic* ups and downs, the Swiss being no exception. But virtually only Switzerland escapes entirely from *political* variation. This removes a big variable that exists in stock markets and one which is so often hard to predict. Swiss political structure is such that even the assassination of its president would hardly be noticed, for he has no great powers, is only elected for a year anyway, and there are no indispensable men in Swiss politics, by virtue of the system.

Investment in Swiss *banks* has proven a wise move for many in recent years. Likewise the *chemical* and *drug* manufacturing business has been a sound area for growth. Information on Swiss company shares is easy to come by, through any Swiss bank. Just to familiarize you with some of the names, in advance, here are a few of the biggest firms: Bally (shoes), Brown-Boveri (machines), Ciba (chemicals and drugs), Geigy (chemicals and drugs), Globus (department stores), Hoffmann-LaRoche (drugs), Internationale Pirelli (cables, rubber), Nestle (food), Suchard Holding (chocolate), and Swissair (airline).

Numbered Accounts

The term "numbered account" always has a romantic ring about it. Some people immediately conjure up pictures of international gangsters slinking into a bank. The stories of Nazis, or the IRS, or the Mafia all rush before one's eyes. However, apart from the fact that the Swiss never knowingly accept "illegal" money, the whole concept of the numbered account is vastly overrated and misunderstood. To begin with, it should be understood how it started. It dates back to the 1930's. The rise of the Nazi party caused many to seek refuge for funds they felt would soon be confiscated. Many families were saved from being wiped out by having this safe and sane sanctuary in mid-Europe. The work and savings of many a lifetime were thus rescued. The same principles apply today.

When a foreigner requests a number-only account he is checked out by some banks, but this varies widely from bank to bank. Some are very fussy; others are not. With some you must have a valid reason, akin to personal danger, as with a dictatorial regime. With these banks tax problems are not a valid reason for such an account. In banks of this kind, number-only accounts held by foreigners are very rare. Others have a more liberal policy. Attitudes change from city to city, bank to bank, month to month.

But number-only accounts for the Swiss themselves are rather common, for reasons of discretion. With so many banks in the country, many citizens have a friend or a cousin working in a bank and they don't want friends or relatives knowing how much salary they earn or how much cash they have or securities held. Unlike Americans who tend to boast about what they earn and hold, the Swiss try to keep it a deep secret. And *all* Swiss communities are very small. This situation causes some people to bank or seek credit in the next town, to keep local people from knowing their business. When people gossip in Switzerland it is (not surprisingly) often about money—other people's.

Investment banks have a higher percentage of number-only accounts than private banks. People from certain countries (e.g. Norway) appear to have a much larger portion of number-only accounts. No one can be sure of such things, but from what I have heard, Americans have very few number-only accounts. The number-only accounts are awkward and generally unneeded for foreigners in Switzerland. They are mostly for psychological reasons, like a fifth padlock on a door.

Of course *all* Swiss accounts have a number, in exactly the same way as an American bank gives you a number. But the secrecy standard in every Swiss bank is sufficiently high as to guarantee absolute secrecy for any account, regardless if it falls within the "numbered" class. However, human beings have been known not to exercise the control required, although divulgence of information by a bank employee is a serious criminal offense in Switzerland. Also mail tampering could occur in the client's country. Hence in this context there is a possible need for a few to have a numbered account. Then the banks simply omit the customer's name on all records, statements, etc. In a special safe, with very limited access, lie the identities of the numbered-account holders.

The customer on the signature specimen card does not write his name but his account number in letters. On all communications with the bank the customer will refer to the account number only and sign his account number in letters instead of his signature. But for 99% of all depositors, the number-only account is unnecessary.

Other arrangements are made, such as coding accounts with names such as "account Alpha" or "account Mexico" or "Rudolph." The letter from the bank to the customer will be signed only by the bank officer, it will be without a letterhead and no reference to the name of the bank or the customer will be made. The envelope will not carry the sender's name or address, or the real name of the recipient.

Should the letter go astray, it will be returned to Switzerland, and then to the bank through the post office which will know the sender by the postage meter number of the stamp. However, some ultra-conservative Swiss institutions go even further and use postage stamps. On request they will even mail letters *outside* of Switzerland. When a password has been agreed on such secret accounts, the teller will refuse acceptance of funds for an account if it is not properly mentioned. Upon specific request the bank will retain all mail for the customer to pick up in person. Also, a special mailing address, valid for certain dates only, may be agreed on.

Regular Name Account

Privacy also prevails here, and because of Swiss banking laws it would be a useless exercise to use one's Swiss bank for reference to, say, a credit card company. However, should such a step be taken by a client, then the bank will divulge nothing until permission from the client has been obtained in writing.

The Joint Account

There are two ways this is handled, usually, when this is a husband-and-wife account. One is where *either* signature is sufficient, and the other where *both* signatures are necessary. In case of the latter arrangement, the only time one signature would suffice would be in the case of death of the other partner. Proof, such as a death certificate, would be required.

Wills

Many customers instruct the bank that a certain person or persons are to have power of attorney over their account in case of their death. This is done because it is obviously simpler for the bank to know within the lifetime of the owner of the account who can act on his/her death. This instruction can be given to the bank on a plain sheet of paper and will be binding upon the bank until the instruction is revoked or replaced by new instructions. Usually the setting up of a beneficiary is handled as follows: The account holder instructs the bank as to the name of the beneficiary. He also instructs a lawyer to inform the bank of his death and the bank in turn informs the beneficiary. It would be necessary to supply the bank with a death certificate, and the bank may request additional evidence to satisfy itself.

Safe Deposit Box

You can have a safe deposit box in a Swiss bank just as you can have one in your own bank at home, and what you put in it is completely up to you. If you keep your stock certificates in it, then you avoid having to pay safekeeping charges from the bank, and only pay the box charge. However, unless you entrust somebody else with the key and an authorization letter, you can never move anything out of the box without a physical visit to the box itself. Some will not even accept authorizations.

Underwriting

Swiss banks are increasingly participating in underwritings of capital issues, of varying sorts and denominations. This includes so-called hot issues of offshore companies or subsidiaries. Many of these issues are denominated in Eurodollars. If you build a good relationship with your Swiss bank, it can get some of the better issues for you.

CHAPTER 9

The Swiss Banker, Saint or Villain?

"It is tough on the Swiss that William Tell should be placed in English folklore by this new image of a gnome in a bank at the end of a telephone line." Andrew Shonfield, 1958

THE expression "gnomes of Zurich," coined by the then British Chancellor of the Exchequer after World War II, when the pound was in trouble, in an attempt to blame somebody, anybody, for the pound's problems, has given the "gnomes" an image that is much larger, both for good and bad, than they deserve.

The Swiss banker is neither saint *nor* villain. He is no different in principle from your banker at home. But he is more sophisticated, more internationally minded, more hip. He is more conservative (i.e. prudent) in his handling of money, and he respects money far more. But the small-town Swiss banker is still just a small-town banker. This aspect of Swiss banking is not generally understood—that while a great deal of publicized high-powered banking goes on (in the manner of international cartels) in Zurich, Basel, and Geneva, there are so *many* Swiss banks that they range all the way down the scale until you find some which are little more than a country store.

However, to the average foreigner, Basel, Zurich, and Geneva are the most likely places where he would deal anyway, so it is the banker in these cities that we are most concerned with in this chapter.

Swiss Bankers Do Not Bring Down Currencies

It must be remembered that Swiss financial operations in many instances are not indicative of the Swiss themselves. If General Motors collapses the cry does not go up

that the brokers forced it down, because it is recognized
that brokers acted on clients' instructions, and it was not
the brokers' place to argue. So it is with Swiss bankers in
most cases. When the "gnomes" are blamed for bringing
down a currency, the image implied is that they all got
together and bear-raided a currency. This is misreporting,
sensational journalism, and invalid. What really happened
was that people all over the world, traders, speculators,
companies, and even ordinary conservative investors,
could see that a particular currency was becoming weak
and ordered their Swiss banker to get them out of it. Many
such clients (most of whom are treasurers of the biggest
international corporations) put standing instructions with
the banks to sell such and such if it gets to a certain price.
Much that is blamed personally on the gnomes is merely
a series of "stop losses" or stop-buys being set off.

However, they affect international economics by means
of the loans they do and do not make. They are in touch
with the flow of much inter-country money and they de-
velop a feel for what is likely to happen next, for what is
relatively safe, and what is seemingly risky. They make
mistakes (like being over-invested in Germany in 1939)
but not many, and not for long. Sometimes they make
judgments that look foolish at the time, like investing in
South Africa in the late 1950's, but when five years later
that showed some of the best gains of the decade, they
suddenly appeared to be farsighted.

Believers in Hard Money

They are generally believers in "hard money" (i.e. conservative money policies by governments) and while their
views on gold vary from banker to banker, in general most
feel it has a crucial part to play in the monetary system and
also in many citizens' portfolios.

They are usually slow to decide, even slower to panic, but hard to stampede and impossible to drive.

They serve as a stabilizing force in world money flow, for they tend not to frighten but to operate by time-tested rules. They believe human nature doesn't change much and thus generally greet new economic theory based on changed human behavior as being unreal and temporary.

The gnome is not a hero, may seem to lack courage and "flair," but in the end he will stand for his beliefs in proven economic doctrine.

He gets the blame for much that is not of his doing, but he also gets credit for much that he has naught to do with.

All in all he's a force for sanity in monetary matters. This must be so or the Swiss banking system would not be the magnificent complex it is.

Swiss Interest in Money

The Swiss banker's great value to the Swiss as a whole and to all those with accounts in Switzerland is that he has only one goal, which confounds many modern new-era thinkers; he keeps ever uppermost in his mind the primary best interests of his *customers*. It is not part of his job to save the pound or be charitable to a starving nation that can't pay its bond issue, or to lose money in order to spread the wealth. His job is to look after the interests of his investors and that he does. This earns him both praise and profanity, but also *respect* for his adherence to principle.

The Swiss banks are institutions unique in the world for their privileged position *vis à vis* their government and *vis à vis* other governments. The Swiss government may not probe a Swiss bank's clients' records. A foreign government has no influence there.

Swiss Secrecy

Swiss law provides for a heavy fine and in addition a six-month jail sentence for violation of its secrecy laws. All employees sign an acknowledgment of these penalties. Violation of secrecy laws also blackballs the offender.

However, it should be noted that tough laws are not generally necessary because Swiss banking is a highly regarded profession and flagrant violation of its own self-governing rules is inherently unthinkable. It has a built-in feeling of responsibility.

Because of long established Swiss neutrality and hundreds of years of keeping faith with depositors through wars and economic crises, Swiss banks enjoy a confidence not in evidence elsewhere. In an uncertain world, Swiss banks seem to offer the nearest thing to certainty and/or safety.

Swiss bankers are not geniuses, not mysterious gnomes. They're just careful (terribly, even tediously careful) men who have a well worn path through the investment wilderness. They are entrusted with great fortunes because they have shown themselves able to fare rather well through good times and bad. They probably perform very few miracles of spectacular appreciation of capital but often just preserving one's capital can be a miracle, during turbulent times. The Swiss don't love money. They respect money, a radically different thing. In respecting it they pursue, handle, and husband money as an end in itself. This is quite different from the emphasis in some countries on things or status symbols. Whether you approve of the Swiss or like their attitude toward life or money is not so important as that their attitude makes Swiss banks a safe harbor for funds in the eyes of millions of investors in countries around the world.

Swiss banks give nothing away. They have a fee for everything, although this often varies with each bank, each branch, each manager, and even each mood, it would seem. But this sometimes annoying and coldly applied fee ritual is strangely satisfying if you realize it is part of a mentality that believes money deserves good attention and good money management or handling deserves a fee. You understand the bank's place in their scheme of things best when you realize that banking is a national industry.

Do Swiss Banks Take Gangster Money?

Swiss banks are not hideouts for Cosa Nostra gangsters' loot. Tabloid Sunday newspapers have given many the impression that because a few notorious deposed dictators and uncouth characters have been rumored to have money (illegally acquired) stashed away in Switzerland that this is virtually the entire purpose of Swiss banking. This should be apparent as both unlikely and intolerable. The Swiss banks take no accounts from people they think might cloud their reputation or cause embarrassment or political complications. Switzerland tries to keep the cleanest image possible for herself. If some stolen money finds its way in, it's by accident.

Who Banks in Switzerland?

Then what sort of people ARE their customers? First there is a growing number of people around the globe whose funds are as international as they think. The money they possess is often changing from currency to currency. They think in terms of the world money market, rather than just their local currency. In this category are included the corporation executives, rich widows, and the oil sheikhs. Perhaps the predominant American business

group is the oil companies, but most big international companies of whatever nationality come into this category and
make full use of the commercial banking facilities that
Switzerland offers.

Of course there is the whole spectrum of people in business, from the giant company which actually keeps offices
in Switzerland (as well as in most major countries in the
world) to the not-so-straightforward import-export companies which are little more than a brass plate on some
Swiss lawyer's office door.

Of the individuals who keep their money in Switzerland
a large group is the Latin Americans, who feel that their
own currencies are not sound enough to leave large sums
of money in, and the very well-to-do oil sheikhs who never
seem to know from one day to the next who will be ruling
their countries. There are no official figures on the size of
the fortunes of these people, but it has been estimated that
up to one billion dollars a year leaves the above-mentioned
countries, and you can be sure that a great deal of it finds
its way into Switzerland. These include the people who use
all of the world's tax havens, from Liechtenstein to the
Bahamas, from Monaco to Jersey, from Malta to the Netherlands Antilles.

But the biggest group of new Swiss depositors in recent
years has been the Americans, of every size estate, making
deposits from $1000 to $1 million. Funds have been fleeing
US shores because of the increasing signs of economic and
monetary deterioration. Balance of payments deficits and
trade deficits and removing gold backing and increasing
restriction of capital flow and limitation threats on travel
funds have all caused many Americans to seek a haven for
some of their funds. Dollar devaluation is seen to be an
eventual inevitability.

Swiss banks are not as unfriendly as they sound in let-

SHOULD KNOW ABOUT SWITZERLAND

ters. They couldn't possibly be. Even if they were jails they couldn't be as unfriendly as their normally cold tone in letters. As the ice drips from their correspondence you must bear in mind that their mother language is not English, and so they can't write it and come across friendly. If you are not Swiss your mother language is not money, so you probably can't speak or understand things in their tongue either. I say this as an American, where business letters are invariably friendly. British depositors may *not* be offended, for business letters in England are also stiff— and the Swiss learned their English from England, not the US.

Many deposed and exiled monarchs do live in Switzerland, and so obviously bank there. In fact some small Swiss towns have telephone directories that read a bit like a *Who's Who.* You find princes doing things like running stores and even becoming stock brokers for branches of American brokerage houses in Switzerland. But these exiled aristocrats are, in most cases, people turned out of their own countries because of revolution, not because they attempted to make off with the national treasury.

Switzerland and Taxes

Much is rumored about the Swiss bank and foreign tax inspectors. The rumors fall into two main types. One says in effect that there is a tax man sitting in the lobby of every Swiss bank taking down details as you walk in. The other says that no foreigner who banks in Switzerland pays any taxes. There is total truth in neither. Presumably tax agents abroad use various methods to try to collect information, although foreign investment and deposits are obviously very difficult to monitor. Swiss banking laws do not give any special privileges to tax inspectors of any nation, mighty or midget, for information gathering. Banking secrecy is banking secrecy. Turn it around for a moment. Supposing you were running a business in the USA, and one of your customers was a foreigner, and this foreign tax authority asked you for information on your client. Would you give it? Even though you are *not* bound by a secrecy law, it's unlikely. In Switzerland there is this *natural* reluctance, plus the law, plus tradition, plus the factor that banking is her biggest business and any threat to its security is equal to a declaration of war. Damage Switzerland's reputation as a safe repository and you do her grievous harm. Thus no amount of yammering by irate politicos will break the barrier.

On the other side, the Swiss are not in business to be the conscience of the world. They cannot afford the time to see that everybody who banks with them pays the correct amount of taxes to their respective governments. Nor do they care. One's tax return in any country is one's own responsibility, and if you don't declare your capital gains from your Swiss shares, or your interest on a bank account then the responsibility rests with you.

The *purpose* of Swiss banks however is certainly NOT for tax evasion. People who insinuate this tend to know so *little* about Swiss banks that this is about the only use they can see for them. But when you realize that a one-stop investment shop, the advantages of a sound currency, of international investment, and greater flexibility are available, then the tax angle diminishes. More about specific taxes later. I might add that this kind of criticism of Swiss banks usually comes from chauvinists, who subconsciously feel anything foreign is bad. When patriotism becomes blind it ceases to be patriotic. I should mention also that I know a great many Americans who have Swiss bank accounts and while they don't show me their tax return, it is clear that most if not all of them have no intention of avoiding any taxes. What they primarily seek in Switzerland are safety of capital and maneuverability, not extra cream off the top.

Swiss banks have also been accused of overthrowing currencies and even governments. While this is violently exaggerated, it is true to say that *indirectly* they can be responsible for the devaluation or revaluation of a currency. When a currency is weak, the speculators do their shorting *through* Switzerland, and so of course this places even greater pressure on the weak currency. However, without the initial weakness, no pressure could be brought to bear. And vice versa regarding revaluation.

The aura of mystery surrounding Swiss banks is in essence the mystery of the Mona Lisa. Calm in the midst of chaos, it is always mysterious. Switzerland has 300 years of internationally recognized neutrality behind her, and when countries are behaving on a national level in a histrionic way, then the Swiss, instead of being caught up in the emotion, are busily looking at the situation from a monetary standpoint, and investing according to logic. The drunk often detests the sober man, and this in essence is the attitude of those who don't understand the Swiss, or Swiss banking.

CHAPTER 10

Switzerland as a Place to Live

"Cleanliness is the most terrifying of all Swiss virtues."   Anon.

WHEN analyzing Switzerland one should begin by stating clearly and unequivocally that there is no such thing as a Swiss, and that in the American concept of a country, there is no such thing as Switzerland.

Facts about Switzerland

Switzerland was incorporated as a country to embrace various small areas which were thought to be too tiny to stand alone. But as there was and still is no all-powerful central government, so the group of states were inflicted with no "national identity."

There are 22 member states speaking four languages (French, German, Italian, and Romansch) and all Swiss people identify with the state (or canton) in which they were born, rather than with Switzerland as a whole. Obviously there are certain characteristics that are national, but these tend to be superficial.

Switzerland basically is a middle class culture. It is politically conservative, regarding socialism and communism as "of the devil." The parliament elects a national president *every year,* which of itself helps preserve freedom, for it allows nobody to be in power long enough to decide he wants more power.

There have been a few famous Swiss in *American* history, for example a group of Swiss settlers in Pennsylvania became the Pennsylvania Dutch, while another Swiss, Albert Gallatin, served Jefferson as his Secretary of the Treasury (a good Swiss occupation!). Yet another Swiss,

John Sutter, first discovered gold in California thus triggering the gold rush of 1848 which changed America's place in the world and altered her structure.

Switzerland is a rather small nation. From about 14,000 feet in the air, on a clear day, it is possible to see the whole country!

It is also the most militaristic state in the world, in the purist sense. *Every* man is a soldier and every inch of the country has a battle plan. Yet the country never goes to war. Every able-bodied man is liable for military service. A major reason they were never attacked is that the invader would find not just an army, but *every* man against him. There is a gun in every house. And yet the Swiss are a peaceful people.

The main characteristics that are common throughout Switzerland are the cleanliness, the efficiency, and a certain clockwork way of running life.

As the cultural areas of Switzerland vary so much, *where*

you decide to live in Switzerland is important. To a degree
you tend to find *simpatico* in areas most near your own
ancestors. Although Americans for example are obviously
more American than anything else, it seems to hold true
that somehow their forefathers' birthplace in Europe
affects the type of European that they can best get along
with. Obviously there are no hard and fast rules, but this
is a guideline. Also whether you come from a small or large
town makes some difference, although one has to remember that in Switzerland everything tends to be in miniature
on US terms.

Their three metropolises, Geneva, Zurich, and Basel,
have city-only populations of between 200,000 and 400,-
000 and Berne (the capital) you would almost miss if you
blinked too slowly passing through. That's a friendly exag-
geration. Of the bigger cities, Geneva seems to be most
able to cope with an English-speaking population, and
there are a number of services and entertainments laid on
simply for the Anglo-American sector. However, English
is understood in all the cities, to some degree, at least in
those sectors of society where the newcomer tends to
make contact.

Therefore if you are contemplating actually living in
Switzerland, part time or full time, you have to deeply
consider which sector suits you, because the three main
areas are like three totally different countries, in atmo-
sphere.

The German Swiss Section

This is the area that most people know best. It tends to
be the area with which the Westerner does his banking. It
stretches from Zurich to Basel, and is thoroughly Germanic in character. The people are the most honest and
honorable in Switzerland (although all Swiss are honest to

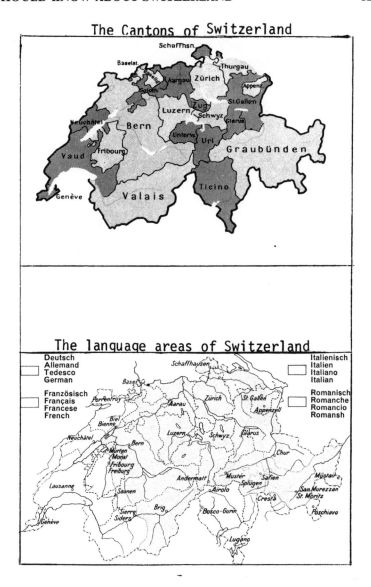

The Cantons of Switzerland

The language areas of Switzerland

a fault; but in the South they bend rules a bit more). Things function like a Swiss watch in this region, from the plumbing to the dry cleaning services. However, the puritan way of life makes the living in this area take on a certain "grey" quality. Pleasant the people may be, and they will not

judge you harshly for slightly more frivolous ways of living, but will rather look on you with interest, as if you had
newly arrived from Mars. The night life in this area is
almost nil. You could shoot a machine gun down the main
street of both Basel and Zurich at 10 P.M. and usually hit
nobody. However, this is the industrial area of Switzerland, albeit industry without smoke, and if you value efficiency, orderly living, and unimaginative kindness and
generosity as among the most important virtues in life,
then this area would suit you.

French Swiss Section

Kingpin of the French Swiss section is Geneva, and this
city has the largest colony of English-speaking people in
Switzerland. Because of this newspapers, radio, social life,
etc., cater to that colony. Hence for the newcomer to
Europe, Geneva has a lot to offer. Perhaps the most irritat-
ing part of Geneva is its large Middle Eastern and Southern European transient labor population and its rather
humid and hot climate in the summer. Throughout the
French section of Switzerland there are many foreign
colonies, for the easier-going attitude of the French Swiss
appeals to many foreigners. Naturally there's more night
life.

Italian Swiss

The only cities of any note in the Swiss Italian sector are
Lugano and Locarno, both beautiful holiday resorts and
tourist centers. For anybody interested in residing in
Lugano, I would suggest he write to Immobiliare, Riva
Caccia 1, Lugano, Switzerland, for their very informative
brochure in English called "Property Purchase in
Lugano." The Italian mentality as a culture in which to live
can be most endearing and at the same time rather frustrat-

A view of Zurich and its famous Fraumunster Church.
Courtesy of the Swiss National Tourist Office

Spring in Lugano, largest city in Italian-speaking Switzerland.
Courtesy of the Swiss National Tourist Office

Geneva and its man-made geyser, the *Jet d'eau*.
Courtesy of the Swiss National Tourist Office

Berne, capital of Switzerland.
Courtesy of the Swiss National Tourist Office

ing. This is also true of Italian Switzerland. There are less rigid restrictions on foreigners here than in the more crowded Germanic North.

Also one might contact Monte Sole, S.A., Via Selva 4, 6900 Lugano-Massagno. This is a modern apartment house project of considerable size organized by Col. Harwood of the American Institute for Economic Research, Great Barrington, Massachusetts, although it is a Swiss corporation and AIER does not own any interest in it. A number of Americans are already living in Monte Sole.

Getting Permission

Throughout Switzerland, if you merely wish to live there for three months at a time, there is no residence problem. Usually two such three-month periods are allowed per year. However, if you wish to live there for a longer period you have to make application to a Swiss consulate or Embassy, and tell them which part of Switzerland you wish to reside in. A lot of foreigners, however, live in Switzerland for three months, leave for the amount of time necessary and then return. This seems to make for a bitty kind of existence but it suits many who wish to spend part of the year in the US or traveling.

The residence applicant will be required to prove that he possesses sufficient means to live in Switzerland without taking up remunerated work. All personal effects can be taken into Switzerland without customs being payable provided you do not sell them within five years of arrival to other Swiss.

Work permits are now either virtually or absolutely impossible to secure. The outlook for the next few years is more of the same. Even so, it's a local canton decision, not a federal one, in each case.

Application will not be accepted unless the applicant has first made a definite choice as to where he wants to live. It helps to be able to produce some names of solid Swiss citizens who will give you a reference. To obtain a Swiss passport, requires a minimum of 12 years' residence and then your case is "considered." Nothing is automatic in Switzerland regarding residency and obtaining Swiss nationality.

Swiss Taxes for Residents

One error many people make when considering Switzerland as a place to live is in assuming that because Switzerland is a corporate tax haven, living there will give them a virtually tax-free life. While tax evasion is *not* a criminal offense, and the tax authorities will negotiate on matters of tax (assuming you obey the law), Swiss taxes are not nearly as comfortable as popular rumor would have you believe.

Outline of Swiss Tax System for Residents

There are three main types of taxes in Switzerland, the Federal taxes, the Canton taxes and the Communal (National, State, and City) taxes. There are no standard rates, as they are levied at progressive rates. Federal Anticipatory Tax and Federal Stamp Duties are levied at flat rates. Other taxes vary radically from canton to canton and from commune to commune, and one tends to find that the best places to live in Switzerland often have the highest taxes!

Federal Taxes

These are applicable to all Swiss residents after six months of residency.

1. Federal Defense Tax

This is levied on:

a) Individuals: total (worldwide) income.

b) Corporations: profits as well as capital and reserves.

For residents the total income from sources inside and outside Switzerland and total capital located in Switzerland and abroad are taxable. There are exceptions for real estate and permanent establishments abroad and the income derived therefrom. No distinction is made whether income is transferred to Switzerland or not.

2. Anticipatory Tax

This is withheld at source mainly on dividends, bond interest, bank interest, and lottery prizes. This tax is also levied against non-residents with money in Switzerland. If a resident you can set this off against your cantonal and communal income. A US citizen resident in Switzerland, can, because of the double taxation treaty, claim this back against his US taxes. Tax rate 30%.

3. Stamp Duties

This is a duty levied on the issue and transfer of securities (shares, bonds, etc.).

Cantonal and Communal Taxes

1. Taxes on income and capital

All 22 cantons (and their communes) of the Swiss Confederation are entitled to levy taxes on income or profit and on capital. Rates vary from place to place. However, the cantons follow more or less the principles set out for the Federal Defense Tax.

The following figures (with U.S. equivalent rates) give some idea of tax burden for residents in Switzerland.

a) Communal and cantonal taxes on *earned income* of 20,000 Swiss Francs in 1965 were:

	Unmarried person	Married person
Zurich	1731 Sw. Fr.	1537 Sw. Fr.
Berne	2042	1858
Geneva	2354	1739
Lausanne	2284	2022
Lucerne	2191	1919

PLUS Federal Defense Tax.
The US tax on equivalent income would be a little over 3000 Francs.
b) The communal and cantonal taxes on *unearned income* for 1965 were, on a capital of 500,000 Fr. with a yield say of 4% (20,000 Fr):

Zurich	3392
Berne	4551
Geneva	3694
Lausanne	5493
Lucerne	5416

plus Federal Defense Tax.

For a man settling in Switzerland as a place to retire, with his only income being that from capital, he can, with the help of a Swiss lawyer, set up a situation whereby he agrees in advance with the tax authorities what his income is and then he pays the pre-agreed sum yearly. However, the amount agreed on has to be a realistic figure, and one on which he can live comfortably. If it isn't then he could suddenly find the Swiss tax man wanting to reassess him based on the lavish party he threw which must have cost half his year's income based on pre-arranged rates.

However, regardless of what status you acquire in Switzerland, while you retain an American passport you are also liable for American taxes, but more on that in the tax chapter.

Map of Switzerland

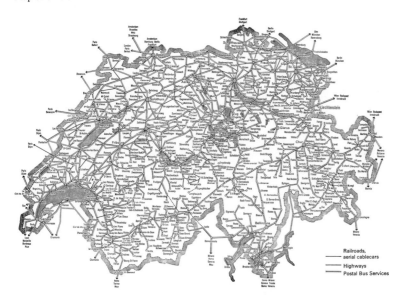

PART 4

Method
(the "How" Factor)

CHAPTER 11

Opening a Foreign Account

"Money is indeed the most important thing in the world; and all sound and successful personal and national morality should have this fact for its basis." George Bernard Shaw

OPENING an account with a foreign bank is similar in most countries. However, *outside* of Switzerland, Americans will find it easier to deal with American banks abroad, rather than trying to open an account long distance with a local bank. The possible exceptions to this rule are foreign banks that are sufficiently big as to have branches in the USA, for example the English bank of Barclays.

Foreign Affiliates of US Banks

The reason it is usually best to stick to foreign affiliates of American banks (outside Switzerland) is that they are used to dealing with Americans, and they know the specific rules and regulations that apply to Americans in the particular country concerned.

For example in England, a nonresident American can open a nonresident account in pounds with an American bank and can take that money out of the country again. However, if he goes to a local bank, and forgets to point out he isn't a resident then the chances are he will find himself with an "internal" account which means to move money, he has to get Bank of England permission. An American bank tends to ask the *right questions* from the start.

This is particularly important in all countries where there is exchange control. However, it isn't true in Switzerland, where no exchange control exists. Although even in Switzerland, for the newcomer to the Swiss banking scene it is generally advisable to stick to the big banking centers of Geneva, Zurich, and Basel, for these places are most accustomed to foreign business and thus able to give you better service.

Mechanics of Opening an Account Abroad

There are a number of methods from which to choose, depending on your personal requirements, how much privacy you wish, and whether you ultimately intend to settle (or spend much time) in the country where you are opening the account.

Here is an assortment of methods, offering various degrees of privacy, and/or ease of action. They are listed in their approximate order of most common use:

1. Just write a personal check on your regular hometown checking account and mail to any bank anywhere in the world with a letter asking them to open an account for you.

2. Buy a bank cashier's check. It can be made out to a bank or (for more privacy) made out to you and endorsed on the back by you to your chosen foreign bank. It can be obtained at your regular bank or at a bank with which you do not normally do business, if you seek greater privacy.

3. You can fly to your chosen foreign bank, carry cash or government bonds and open an account in person.

4. You can make a direct bank transfer. That is you merely instruct your local bank to make a transfer of funds from your account to the chosen bank abroad, and they do the rest.

5. You can go to a branch of a Swiss bank in certain other countries, and of course you can get help from the local US bank that has a foreign branch, but obviously, even with the Swiss branch, Swiss banking law is not fully in force outside Switzerland.

6. You can send 91-day US Government Treasury Bills (or government bonds of whatever country you live in) which are made out to bearer, as your deposit. Seldom done.

7. You can give a deposit to a Swiss bank messenger in whichever countries he operates. But this is more Hollywood imagery than common practice. It is both very rare and usually done only by "marginal" banks.

Foreign Brokerage Houses

Generally, you would be well advised not to try to buy and sell stock direct through a foreign brokerage house. Its concept of information is quite different, as is its scale of commissions. Nearly all foreign markets work on a "bid and ask" price system for ALL stocks, even the biggest, and trying to get intelligible statements out of them is well nigh impossible, especially when the country of origin is not English-speaking. It is easier to use the brokerage facilities of a Swiss bank for all foreign stock transactions.

US Brokerage Houses Abroad

Many of the bigger US brokerage houses have branches abroad. However, these are not provided so that Americans can trade foreign stock, but rather so that foreigners and Americans abroad can trade US stock. They are little islands of America in the midst of an alien city. Facilities are usually very good, and quotes and orders can be gotten almost as fast as in the US. When traveling abroad, a local branch of *any* US brokerage house (not just the one you deal with at home) will usually take your orders on a give-up basis. However, most of them operate primarily to transmit foreign *bank* orders to the U.S.

Communications with the Bank

Once you have opened your account it is best (if you can) to establish communications with one person only in the bank, and then use this person to cope with errors, questions, misunderstandings, etc. that are bound to arise. Without this the world of the Swiss bank is often completely incomprehensible to the layman. You will have to ask for a name as their signatures are never legible, by design. Not all banks will accommodate your request. All Swiss banks communicate in three languages. Most statements and formal documents are printed in two or three languages, or sometimes even in four, depending on which language area the bank is in. German is *always* found. French is common. Italian is less common. English is spasmodically used. The problem is that when the Swiss write a letter, or send out a form or a circular letter, the chances are that they will choose the wrong language for you, and nothing is more frustrating than to receive what appears to be a notice or data or a form of vital importance in a language you can't begin to read. So always request they send everything in English. Most communications from a Swiss bank come signed by two people. This is required procedure for their banks. Also, when you do raise questions, their letters of reply are stiff and in a form of English that you have to read several times to make sure you fully understand. These problems can be lessened to some degree if you open an account with an American bank in Switzerland, where they are used to dealing with Americans. Under Swiss law some foreign banks have subsidiaries which are chartered as Swiss banks. Examples: Chase, American Express, and United California Bank, which are actually Swiss banks in their own right, and operate with the same rules of privacy and self-containment as any totally Swiss bank. The rest operate as pure branches and not separate banks, like Bank of America, First National City, and Morgan Guaranty.

Communication also is a little slower than in the US, partly of course because of the time it takes for a letter to cross the Atlantic, and partly because the Swiss work at a slightly less frantic pace than the Americans. But here again speed is linked to national characteristics. You get faster service from the German Swiss than from the French Swiss or Italian Swiss. Statements are normally issued by Swiss banks every quarter, and it is well to have them explained at the outset, for they are very different from US statements. Also, after establishing which language you require for communication, it does no harm to repeat it occasionally.

Power of Attorney

Swiss banks operate via power of attorney on accounts should you so desire. But like anybody else you give power of attorney to, they do not promise a one-way street to riches. If, however, you buy foreign stock or foreign "paper" then it is often better to let them decide when it should be sold. But there are a few cautionary points before giving a Swiss bank your power of attorney.

1. The Swiss method of trading is quite different from the US. They, like most Europeans, buy on rumor, or "inside information" and hold until the stock gets to where they were advised it will go, ignoring fluctuations in the middle. They also ignore charts, as a rule. This is most unlike your US broker relationship; when things go down you can't as conveniently pick up your telephone and have a consoling talk, so you have to program yourself to be able to live with this.

2. As you can trade on less margin than in the US, you can

find yourself answering a margin call much faster than you
are used to and of course can become far more overex-
tended.

3. Swiss traders (in the bank's investment department),
while being quite sound in most instances, have a nearly
total verbal blind spot to a *discussion* of a decision they
have made. Especially the Germans. They cannot for the
life of them see why, if you have allowed them to buy a
stock, you should periodically wish to review their reasons. They come over as stubborn and dogmatic and this
can be most frustrating if your foreign stock is down, and
you would like some comfort. So you have to prepare for
this in advance. In their defense one might say that longer-
term traders tend to make more profits than in-and-outers.

4. It is well to lay down very clear guidelines initially
when giving a bank power of attorney such as, whether or
not you are willing to trade on margin, whether or not you
are willing to trade in commodities, what countries you
will and will not be willing to hold stock in, whether or not
the bank has your permission to renew contracts, or interest-bearing paper, etc. without consulting you first,
whether to call you for more margin or just take it from
your account, and so forth. Obviously most of these points
apply equally to giving your local broker power of attorney
but with the Swiss bank you are dealing from a distance
and with a foreign mentality and in battered English. Thus
misunderstandings can arise.

Also statements of trading activities are very different
from the US broker's statement so you should get these
explained at the outset. Often you don't know if you
bought or sold or got a dividend. It is well to visit your
bank from time to time, and it will willingly explain queries
you have, and deal with your problems. You will find it
much cheerier in person than on paper.

Which Bank—a List of possibilities

Switzerland: After five years of operation a bank domiciled in Switzerland may apply for membership in the Swiss Bankers Association. This body was founded to protect the interests of its members. It enters into gentlemen's agreements with the Central Bank, generally informs the member banks on various topics of mutual interest, briefings on bank legislation and conventions for the uniform treatment of certain business and its remuneration. One of the prerequisites for acceptance in this association is a clean record of conduct for the applicant bank during the initial five years of its operation. It would therefore be good for a customer's peace of mind to know that his Swiss banker is a member of this association, or (if under five years old) is otherwise known to have a good reputation.

Among the more prominent associates are the following:

Swiss Bank Corporation
Aeschenvorstadt 1
4000 Basel

Union Bank of Switzerland
Bahnhofstrasse 45
8000 Zurich

Swiss Credit Bank
Paradeplatz
8000 Zurich

All of these (above) have branches throughout Switzerland, and agencies abroad in such places as New York and London.

Bank Leu & Cie
Bahnhofstrasse 32
8000 Zurich—this is a large bank among the small ones

Schweizerische Volksbank (People's bank)
Bahnhofstrasse 53
8000 Zurich—it has branches throughout Switzerland

Private Banks

Julius Baer & Cie
Bahnhofstrasse 36
8000 Zurich

Dreyfus Sohne & Cie
Aeschenvorstadt 14-16
4000 Basel

Ehinger & Co
Aeschenvorstadt 15
4000 Basel

Lombard Odier & Cie
Rue Corraterie 11
1200 Geneva—handles large private investment accounts

Pictet & Cie
Rue Diday 6
1200 Geneva—accepts no account under $50,000

A Sarasin & Cie
Freie Strasse 107
4000 Basel

Troillet & Cie
Rue Bovy-Lysberg 17
1200 Geneva

J. Vontobel
Bahnhofstrasse 3
8000 Zurich

There are several foreign banks in Switzerland: Russian, American, Israeli, Arab, French, English, Scandinavian and Italian. That is, I think, a complete list. And the attitude of the Swiss government is one of not quite prohibiting new ones but certainly discouraging them. The 1969 banking laws were less liberal in this respect. This applies also to takeovers by foreigners of existing banks, i.e. not impossible but nearly so. Policies change from time to time, of course.

It is interesting to note, in passing, that there are no German banks in Switzerland and no Swiss banks in Germany. It would seem to be more than coincidence; a gentlemen's agreement is assumed to exist. . . . To advertise Swiss banks abroad, with emphasis on their Swiss-ness, is also now discreetly discouraged.

Of the affiliates of foreign banks in Switzerland there are two main types:

1. Those that are truly foreign *branches* and therefore are subject to their main office (wherever the main office is), and

2. Those that, although they bear the name of their foreign head office, are truly Swiss banks by charter. A complete list is impractical to include here, but a complete list of US banks is appropriate.

The *true* Swiss banks (though subsidiaries) are:

American Express, at

> 20 Streitgasse, Postfach 1108, Basel
> 7 Rue du Mont Blanc, Case Postale 243, Geneva
> Hotel du Rhone, Quai Turrettini, Geneva
> 14 Av. Mon-Repos, Case Postale 1653, Lausanne
> Schweizerhofquai 4, Postfach 1146, Lucerne
> 58 Grand Rue, Case Postale 232, Montreux
> Bahnhofstrasse 20, Postfach 758, Zurich.

Chase Manhattan Overseas Banking Corp., Rue du Rhone 114, Geneva.

Those that are simply branch offices of their parent company:

First National City Bank, St. Peterstrasse 16, Zurich

> Rue du Rhone 100, Geneva
> 43 Rue de Bourg, P.O.B. 1002, Lausanne
> 9 Corso Pestalozzi, P.O.B. 6901, Lugano

Bank of America   Borsenstrasse 16, Zurich

Morgan Guaranty Trust   Stockerstrasse 38, Zurich

These branches are of course still subject to Swiss law.

American banks also have branches in many other countries, of course. There is in fact no major city in the world without a US bank. In London there are 30, which makes it unique for probably only New York exceeds London in its variety of American banks.

Many banks claim to have, or appear to claim to have, a branch in Switzerland, when in fact they have only a representative office (like Continental Illinois National Bank and Trust), or they simply have correspondent banks—which means little more than an agreement between non-related banks to cooperate with each other on certain banking matters.

Swiss Banks Abroad

Likewise, Swiss banks have branches in many cities of the world. For example Swiss Bank Corporation has a full office in San Francisco, two in New York and two in London. It has representative offices in Beirut, Buenos Aires, Hong Kong, Johannesburg, Lima, Los Angeles (510 W. 6th St., Suite 532), Madrid, Mexico, Paris, Rio de Janeiro, Sao Paulo, Sydney and Tokyo. Further it has subsidiaries in Panama, Nassau, Casablanca, Montreal, and Toronto. Within Switzerland it has offices in 70 cities, from Aarau and Aigle to Zug and Zurich. See the Appendix for a full list of foreign addresses.

CHAPTER 12

Problems and How to Overcome Them

"If the Romans had been obliged to learn Latin, they would have never found time to conquer the world." Heinrich Heine

PERHAPS the biggest problem that faces the international investor is that of language, firstly because in many countries where there are excellent investment opportunities the language is not English, and secondly because in countries where they do speak English, they neither write nor think in English, let alone American.

Anybody who studies languages will know that it is almost impossible to translate from one language to another, word for word, and have it come out in precisely the same meaning in both languages. The reasons for this are that the construction of languages varies, and, as we all think in words our thought patterns from country to country are as dissimilar as our language structures. An example of this is Japan which has a language constructed like building blocks, with nothing flowery, nothing poetic about it. This gives the Japanese an intensely practical (geometric if you like) thought pattern. It is uncertain which came first; presumably the geometric thought patterns came first and a language was devised which had no need for abstract shades of meaning, in the way the French language has for example. In French, a man can write you the most flowery letter, full of humilities, niceties, flourishes of language, and overly formal addresses when in fact he is threatening to sue you if you don't pay the bill you owe him.

Because of this vast difference in language, few people

ever *really* learn another language completely. Oh yes, they may write or speak it well enough to be understood, but generally they still *think* in their own language. This means that as an American trying to communicate with, say, a British organization, the stiffness, the "heretofores" and the "aforesaids" will drive you mad. Worse still, you will each *assume* different things based on different cultures. When communicating with the Swiss who have learned English from the English (not the Americans), you not only get the formality of English English, but you also get the coldness that German has. The Swiss *are* extremely friendly people, but even in person, as an American I find I have to constantly remind myself to pay more attention to what they do than to what they say. Perhaps they in turn find me crude, and maybe even ill-mannered because of my informal American approach and American directness.

This may be a long way of saying: When communicating with a foreign bank try to see *what* they say, not how they say it, and when writing yourself, keep sentences short, concise, and don't meander or succumb to the American habit of assuming that one has to be rude (or at least forceful) in a business letter to get action. We grow up accepting communication by not only meanings but "shades of meaning." So when we do business with foreigners for the first time, the difference in communication, and in some instances the resulting breakdown in communication, is horrifying. Remember that unless you are one of those rare birds who know several languages, THEY will be coming out to meet you by attempting to communicate in YOUR language, so make it as easy as possible, and don't expect the impossible (i.e. flawless dialogue).

It's just not practical to pick up a phone and call your Swiss bank or foreign broker for a chat or quotes. Apart from the cost, time difference and transcontinental problems, a foreign accent always comes out *more* foreign on a telephone, and the chances are you or he wouldn't understand some key word. So you have to be able to get information on what you buy, sell, and trade by other means. A Swiss or other foreign bank or broker will mail you confirmations on all trades. But as they look very different, I'm picturing some of the common forms used. While this gives you a start, for your own peace of mind you should, when you open an account abroad, have somebody explain all the statements, confirmation slips, what all the columns mean, what the charges are, how they work. It isn't that they are not to be trusted, but it saves discontent later,when you find, say, 5% added on a bill and then they insist it is normal. You rave, they become irate, and it could have all been avoided if you had discovered at the outset the double or triple commission plus safekeeping or storage charge would amount to this (if you have done something quite complicated). As the Swiss are slower to insult one another than are Americans, they take it more bitterly than fellow Americans when you insult them, and you could lose a lot of your cooperation by such episodes.

As to receiving quotes on foreign stocks: There are several newspapers that one can subscribe to on a daily or weekly basis to get foreign stocks. The best of course is the *Financial Times,* Bracken House, Cannon Street, London E.C.4, England. This publication arrives in most places in the USA no more than a day later, and contains quotes and news on all British stocks, South African, Malaysian, Australian, Canadian, US shares and a smattering of others. For *professionals* there are three Swiss papers covering prices only (no news) of the Swiss stocks on their three exchanges (most that you would want would be in the Zurich paper). These are *Schweizerischer Bankverein* (in German), Art.Instutut Orell Fussli AG, Postcheck-Konto 80-640, Zurich; the *Geneva Journal of the Borse* (in French), and the *Basel Kursblatt* (in German) both put out by the Swiss Bank Corporation in the respective cities. They all also give prices on those foreign stocks which are listed in Switzerland's exchanges. For non-professionals by far the best coverage is in the *Neue Zuricher Zeitung* (two editions a day) which carries news as well as prices. News in German of course. Available on leading newsstands throughout the world. At first, some of the confirmation slips one receives from a foreign bank can make you gasp. This is because once you start thinking internationally, not only is the whole procedure more complicated than banking round the corner and using a broker across the street, but often it is necessary for preliminary things to happen in order that WHAT you want can be done. For example you decide to buy some Suchard, nothing more. Suddenly you get a confirmation slip showing somebody somewhere wrote a huge check on your account. Later on quite a different colored or shaped piece of paper you will get confirmation of the stock purchase. You may also possibly receive confirmation that somebody somewhere wrote *you* a huge check for something or other. If so, what has happened is that in order to buy this foreign stock from your dollar account (if you have one) you had to buy some Swiss Francs first in order to purchase the stock. This means the bank has to show your losing the dollars, gaining the Francs, and *then* buying the stock. The reverse happens when you sell. You will also find yourself, with very little effort, with a *number* of accounts when you thought you only had one. This is because every time you want to do something different the chances are there will be a new account opened. For example you now have your dollar account and your Swiss Franc account with the Suchard. You then want to buy some German marks, just because you like the design on them (or their parity), and then you have a D-mark account. Then you would like to trade on margin, for futures, etc., so you then have a margin account and so forth. The more accounts, the more errors can occur. Even bankers are human, so do check all your transactions WHEN they occur, not six months later.

In *dwelling* on problems I may have discouraged you. But actually it should be encouraging, for with these guidelines it is unlikely anything can surprise you or go wrong. You should be able to act with *confidence* as a result of knowing all the pitfalls that neophytes fall into. And it's not so complicated as it may sound; rather it's the newness that makes anything unknown seem like more than it is. The FIRST Swiss bank statement may puzzle but from then on it's all downhill. Further, it's no more complicated than one's own banking system; the difference is that one is already a known factor. Also, it's educational, helps you understand how international economics works, broadens your horizon.

Investment Letters

As an afterthought to the above, it occurs to me that you may find considerable help, guidance and ideas from certain investment letters which attempt to cover all or much of the international scene. Many letters touch on it but only a handful make any serious effort to provide worldwide advice. I would mention these:

1. *International Bank Credit Analyst* (1245 Sherbrooke

St. West, Montreal), $275 a year, does a good monthly *technical* analysis of most world markets.

2. *Standard & Poor's International Stock Report* (345 Hudson St., New York, NY), $40 a year, provides *fundamental* information about 21 individual (different) foreign shares each month.

3. *Investment Research,* 36 Regent Street, Cambridge, England. It does a quick technical rundown on most foreign markets plus the New York and London markets in detail.

4. *International Harry Schultz Letter* (Suite 226, 67 Younge St. Toronto, Canada, M5E1J8, or P.O. Box 1161, Basel 4002, Switzerland), $177 a year. I don't list my own advisory letter here without just cause. *HSL* has an outstanding record in forecasting stock market movements throughout the world, with special emphasis on the London and New York markets. Shares are also recommended. Additionally *HSL* produces sections on international economics and USA economics, as well as the largest coverage on gold of any newsletter, plus a small section on silver, and currency and monetary analysis. (My current private address is: 170 Sloane Street, London SW.1.)

Bank Statement Illustrations

I intended at this point to insert a number of examples of Swiss bank statements and routine reports that are issued to clients, so I approached a number of banks for permission to print their forms with fictitious names and figures on them. I pointed out that it would be good publicity for their banks. I met polite but blanket refusal. It seemed to matter little whether the bank was small or large; they just were not willing to allow even the slightest infringement on their privacy or methodry. They didn't seem to care about publicity. But part of their sacred "parchments" *should* be displayed to public eye. I have therefore made up a composite statement from several banks, in order to give you some idea of what a Swiss bank statement looks like. As far as we know you will find none like this in Switzerland, although some will be similar.

SCHULTZBANK

ZURICH

99999
Bill Jones, New York

Börse / Stock Exchange / Bourse

Ihrem Auftrag zufolge haben wir für Sie VERKAUFT
In accordance with your instructions we have SOLD for you
Selon vos instructions, nous avons VENDU pour vous   11.2.69

Titel/Security/Titre: AKT. CLEVITE CORP.

Nominal / Stück Nominal / Number Nominal / Nombre	Kurs Price Cours	Kurswert Gross value Montant brut	./. Courtage Commission	./. Stempel, Gebühren Stamps, fees Timbres, taxes	./. Spesen Expenses Frais	Netto zu Ihren Gunsten Net Credit Net à votre crédit Fr.	Wert Value Valeur
100	80,00	$8000,00	35,25		47,00	$7917.75	11.1.69

☐ Die Titel entnehmen wir Ihrem Depot.
   We withdraw the securities from your custody-account.
   Nous prélevons les titres de votre dépôt.

☐ Die Titel wollen Sie uns bitte zustellen.
   Please send us the securities.
   Veuillez nous faire parven r les titres.

Hochachtungsvoll / Yours faithfully / Vos dévoués

Zs = Zins seit / Interest from / Intérêt du

SCHULTZBANK

ZURICH

Bill Jones
New York

99999

r bitten Sie, diese Abschlussrechnung sowie den beigelegten Kontokorrentauszug zu prüfen
d uns die beiliegende Richtigbefundsanzeige baldmöglichst unterschrieben zurückzusenden.

us vous prions de signer l'avis de bien-trouvé ci-joint et de nous le retourner aussi vite que possible.

ase check this status of your account as well as the enclosed statement and give us your agreement
signing and returning to us the attached acknowledgement.

	Konto-Nummer No de compte Account No.		Abschluss per Arrêté au Closed per		Währung Monnaie Currency	
30 JUN69		99999		30.06		
					Zu Ihren Lasten En notre faveur In our favour	Zu Ihren Gunsten En votre faveur In your favour
r Saldo / Solde précédent / Old balance						7,2383.17
Sollzins / 1er int. débiteur / 1st debit int.			% a/			
Sollzins / 2me int. débiteur / 2nd debit int.			% a/			
enzins / Int. créancier / Credit Int.		4.00	% a/	7,077		78.60
rechnungssteuer / Impôt anticipé / Withholding tax		30.00	% a/	78.60 *	23.60	
m. a. Soll-U satz / Comm. s. mut. débiteur / Comm. on debi turnover			% a/			
m. vom höchsten Soll-Saldo/Comm. s. le solde déb. max./Comm. on highest debit bal.			% a/		1.17	
sen / Frais / Charges						
				30.06	24.77	
tal / Totale	Wert / Valeur / Value					
uer Saldo / Nouveau solde / New balance						7337.00

= Verrechnungssteuerpflichtiger Betrag
  Montant soumis à l'impôt anticipé
  Amount subject to withholding tax

Hochachtungsvoll / Vos devoués / Yours faithfully

SCHULTZBANK

ZURICH

Coupons

Dividend - Advice

Bill Jones, New York

99999

Wir erkennen Sie, Eingang des ungekürzten Betrages vorbehalten:
Sous réserve de la rentrée du montant intégral, nous créditons votre compte:
We have credited your account, subject to receipt of proceeds:

13.11.69

Gattung / Titre / Security		Nom./Anzahl/Nombre/Number	Coupons à
AKT. WELCOME GOLD MINING CO. LTD		3560	1/5, 5

Verfall/Echéance/Due	Brutto/Brut/Gross	Steuer/Impôt/Tax	%	Kommission/Spesen Comm./Frais/Charges	Netto/Net/Net	Kurs/Cours/Rate
7.11	£259/11/8	38/18/9	15	3/17/11	£216/15/0	10, 340

Doppelbesteuerungsabkommen Schweiz / USA. Falls rückforderungsberechtigt, kann mit dieser Abrechnung folgender Betrag geltend gemacht werden.

Convention de double imposition Suisse / USA. Si qualifié au remboursement, le montant suivant peut être récupéré avec cet avis de crédit:

Doubletaxation agreement Switzerland / USA. If entitled to reimbursement, the following amount can be claimed with this credit advice:

Gutschrift/Crédit/Credit	Valuta/Valeur/Va
2 241.20	10 Nov

Fr.

Hochachtungsvoll / Vos dévoués / Yours faithfully

Anzeige ohne Unterschrift / Avis sans signature / Advice without signature

Bill Jones
New York

SCHULTZBANK

ZURICH

Devisen / Service des Changes
Foreign Exchange Department

March 16th, 1970

Wir kauften von Ihnen / Nous vous avons acheté / We have bought from you:

US-$2000.00 .... Val. Mar 16, 70   Kurs cours rate 4.33 .... — sfrs 8'660.00 .... Val. Mar 16.

zu Ihren Gunsten E. v.
en votre faveur s. b. f. / In your favour u. u. r.

Vergütung / bonification / remittance

US-$ Margin Account No. 99999
Cash for stock purchase

Ref.

sfrs - account no. 99998

Hochachtungsvoll / Vos dévoués / Yours faithfully

SCHULTZBANK AG

ZURICH

Rechnungs-Auszug für
Relevé de compte pour
Statement for

Bill Jones
New York

Depositenkonto
Compte de dépôt
Deposit Account

Blatt Nr./Feuille No/Page No.

Konto-Nr./No.de compte/Account No.
Abschluss per./Arrêté au/Closed per
1. Soll-Zinssatz/1er taux int. débiteur/1st debit int. rate
Limite für 1. Soll-Zins/Limite pour 1er taux débit./Limit of 1st debit int. rate
2. Soll-Zinssatz/2me taux int. débiteur/2nd debit int. rate
Haben-Zinssatz/Taux int. créancier/Credit int. rate
Komm. u. Spesen/Comm. u. frais débiteur/Comm. on debit turnover
Komm. vom höchsten Soll-Saldo/Comm. le solde déb. maximum/Comm. on highest debit balance
Kreditlimite/Limite de crédit/Limit of credit
Deckung/Garantie/Collateral

Datum Date	Text Texte Description	Code	Wert Valeur Value	Währung/Monnaie/Currency		Saldo/Solde/Balance	Tage Jours Days	Zinsnr.-Saldo/nomb. d'int./interest numbers	
				Soll/Débit/Debit	Haben/Crédit/Credit			Soll/Débit/Debit	Haben/Crédit/Credit
DEZ 19	$3000 check USA		19.12		3000.00	3000.00	82	0	3000.00

Codes : 1 = Frankoposten/Mouvement franco/free of commission
2 = Abschlussbuchung/Ecriture de bouclement/summary of closing status

Bemerkungen/Observations/Remarks

Buchungen nach dem Abschlussdatum erscheinen in neuer Rechnung
Les opérations effectuées après la date de clôture apparaîtront sur le prochain relevé
Entries after closing date appear on new statement

* = Saldo zu Ihren Gunsten / Solde en votre faveur / **Balance in your favour**
D = Saldo zu Ihren Lasten / Solde à votre débit / **Balance to your debit**

CHAPTER 13

U S Taxes on Foreign Income for U S Citizens

"The Art of Taxation consists in so plucking the goose as to obtain the largest amount of feathers with the least amount of hissing." Jean Baptiste Colbert

THIS chapter is not intended to be the sort of advice given you by an accountant or tax lawyer, but merely a basic tax outlook on foreign investments and living abroad. It is always advisable to seek help when attempting to do anything out of the ordinary taxwise. And the time to seek help is BEFORE you put wheels in motion, rather than after income is generated and potential tax exposure created.

I propose to concentrate in this chapter on what taxes the US government levies on foreign investments, both on Americans living inside the USA and on Americans living abroad. It would take too long to list the tax laws of the various European countries here, but I would suggest that you contact the embassy of any country you intend to consider moving to for tax information. I would also recommend a short book on European taxes, which outlines each country in turn and its setup. It is: *Taxation in Western Europe,* price 35/- ($4.36) from Confederation of British Industry, 21 Tothill Street, London S.W.1, England. This little book gives, very simply, the tax structure of 17 European countries, and such information as double taxation relief. It is written mainly for a British market, so it's not complete for Americans, but it is a very good beginning if you are contemplating living or creating a company or spending considerable time in a Western European country.

An American Living Abroad and US Taxes

First of all there are certain classes of US citizens abroad that do not qualify for any exemptions, and for all practical purposes are treated as if they were still within the USA. These are US government employees and employees of the US Armed Forces and US citizens abroad with only unearned income. However, these two categories have certain rules of their own whereby some of their allowances have certain concessions. But in this book we are mainly concerned with the ordinary civilian American. The exemption laws do however apply to employees of US companies abroad, as well as all other American employees who may qualify for exemption of income earned abroad. The law talks of "income from non-US sources," and this is confusing, for by this is meant the place where the service is performed, not where it is paid. In other words you are entitled in certain circumstances to the income exemption if you are physically resident in a foreign land, even though the money you are paid may technically come from within the USA. Of the situations where Americans are resident abroad, there are special laws for Americans living in Puerto Rico, the Virgin Islands and US protectorates which do not apply to residence in the rest of the world.

The exemptions allowable to US citizens living abroad only apply to earned income, not to unearned income. Even if you have no property in the US and receive no income from US sources you are still liable for US taxes. This is, in my view, unfair and highly discriminatory. No other nation seeks to tax its citizens when they live elsewhere and get no benefits for taxes paid. But until some wise Solons change it, this is indeed the law. As a United States citizen living and working (or retired) abroad with the exceptions mentioned above, your first $20,000 income is tax-free. This exemption rises to $25,000 after three years. However, this isn't quite as good as it sounds, for remember, to qualify as a foreign resident you will de facto be paying the local taxes of the country in which you are living AS WELL AS US TAXES. Normally you end up paying taxes in both places, and then having to claim one against the other. You usually end up paying the higher of the two.

When taking up residence abroad, there is a situation where your residence is not necessarily your domicile, and this will have an effect usually on your local taxes. Your residence is where you are living. Your domicile is where your home really is and where you ultimately hope to return. If you are not domiciled in a foreign country, there may be certain tax concessions allowable to you on local taxes. The IRS puts out a publication called "Tax Guide for US Citizens Abroad" which is essential reading for anybody wishing to take up temporary or permanent residence abroad.

An American Living in the USA with Foreign Income

Foreign taxes on foreign income are usually deducted at source. This means when you get your dividends from foreign stock, the foreign tax has already been taken, in most cases. In order to avoid paying taxes AGAIN to the US you can claim this tax against your federal income tax. You can claim this as a *deduction,* or as a *credit,* the latter normally more advantageous. In either case the full amount of the dividend before withholding must be included on US income tax returns.

Currencies

For tax purposes, trading currency is regarded as a capital asset and generally taxed by the same rules as securities.

Interest Equalization Tax

Certain acquisitions by United States citizens are subject to the Interest Equalization Tax. Generally all foreign investments acquired from a foreigner are liable to this tax, although there are certain investments, for example certain new Canadian issues and investments in less developed country corporations, that are exempt. The tax is payable whether you acquire the securities in the US or through a foreign broker or banker. In the case of acquisition through a foreign broker or banker, it is the individual's obligation to report this. The foreigner will not do this for you. If you acquire the foreign share in the US through a US broker then he must by law file with the IRS that you have bought this stock, although he will not pay the income tax for you "at source." US brokers in branches abroad buying for US citizens must also file this. It is still up to you to file details of IE purchases when you file your tax return. The tax does not apply to certain investments under one year (hence certain foreign certificates of deposit are set up to expire in 364 days).

Interest Equalization Tax—What It Is

This is a unique tax in that it is *not* a tax on *income* in any form in the normal sense. It is an excise tax, a penalty tax or exchange control fee imposed on acquisition of the foreign security and if you lose money in that security the tax is STILL paid. It is not deductible against another tax, and is usually treated simply as part of the purchase price of a foreign security.

The tax varies from .79% to 11.25% depending on the type of foreign investment and when you bought it. Stocks bought from another American on "ADR" (American depository receipt) are not subject to this tax, as the tax has already been paid once and there is a certificate showing this. The IET is an indirect form of exchange controls, and is as unpopular as any tax since the Boston Tea Party.

Swiss Taxes Imposed at Source on Investments Held by Foreigners (USA, etc.)

The only taxes payable in Switzerland by a foreigner holding only a bank account there are those deducted by the banks at the source. These are the 30% withholding tax on the credit interest payments 25% of which is recoverable in cash from the Swiss government on the basis of the Swiss-American double taxation agreement. Also recoverable in full is the 30% withheld on US stock dividends in the form of a tax credit on the annual 1040 income tax return. As a logical consequence of his filing with the Swiss government, the US claimant should report the dividend or interest income on his own tax return. No capital gains or income taxes are levied in Switzerland on non-residents in connection with bank accounts held there.

Any "ADR" bought by a foreigner including a Swiss or other foreign bank regardless of possible Interest Equalization Tax clearance (i.e. regardless of whether at some time it had become an ADR) automatically becomes "foreign" when the bank purchases it. Therefore a Swiss bank cannot legally purchase ADR domestic stock for a US customer unless a subaccount in the name of the US customer, stating his full identity (Social Security number), is maintained by the Swiss bank with an American bank or broker. Swiss banks do not open such accounts without special written instructions from the client.

Tax Havens

In recent years the term "tax haven" is increasingly in the news. A tax haven is a place that has little or no local tax, although sometimes the lower the local tax the less stable is the political structure of the place. Because of worldwide taxation policy of the US government on individual citizens, the actual saving for the individual through a tax haven is a lot less than would be imagined on the surface. However, there are a number of corporate structures that can be made in tax havens that do benefit the taxpayer, and which are perfectly legal. Such structures obviously have to be worked out with a competent lawyer or accountant. Physical presence of capital in the tax haven chosen is not always necessary, if the structure setup is merely a "shell" for operations elsewhere, and so in this sense political instability can be overcome. However, the IRS may treat US-controlled foreign corporations as a sham in the absence of any commercial substance.

Some places are obviously more welcoming than others, and offer a fiscally mild climate but in structuring anything through a tax haven, not only must one consider the full ramifications of US taxes, but if the structure is to be used for any sort of business operation, then the reputation of the particular haven must be weighed as a factor in the business. If the haven is too "shady," then, however honest your business, it de facto may have a shady image, which could hurt. The best-known tax havens are the Bahamas, Liechtenstein, Bermuda, Gibraltar, Malta, Curacao, Cayman, Channel Islands, and some would say Switzerland, but the last being the most sound is less fiscally welcoming than the others (e.g. corporate taxes are 30%, hardly a free ride).

Sum Up

The foregoing has, I hope, served especially to give you a summary of the tax aspects involved when living or investing abroad as a US citizen or both. As stated earlier, if you intend to reside abroad, or invest substantially, or consider a foreign corporation, it is best to find a qualified accountant, preferably with an international firm who has branches in the US as well as in the country where you reside. Otherwise you may find you are either subject to penalties (even if through innocence) or overlapping taxation, or at minimum simply not getting all the advantages that are possible.

CHAPTER 14

A Different Language and Culture "Them and Us"

"They spell it Vinci and pronounce it Winchy; foreigners always spell better than they pronounce." Mark Twain, in *Innocents Abroad*

THE stranger (especially the English-speaking stranger) feels as if he's getting mail from the Moon when he gets correspondence from his Swiss bank.

The mixture of language and abbreviations are so baffling that at first often up to 50% of the communication may be beyond one's comprehension.

These hints will help: be sure to tell your bank to reply in English and send your banking notices on English forms. Tell them you cannot read German, French, or Italian. Keep this list of common abbreviations handy which are used endlessly by them, on forms, confirmations and statements.

German	French	English
Depotgebuhren	*droits de garde*	safekeeping
Jahr	*anée*	year
Schweiz	*Suisse*	Switzerland
Wertstellung,	*valeur*	value or date
Valuta, Wert		(when transaction effective)
Ausland	*étranger*	abroad
Soll	*debit*	debit
Konto Nr.	*no. de compte*	account number
Haben	*credit*	credit
(Borsen)-	*courtage*	stock exchange
Kommission		commission
Stempel und Gebuhren	*timbre et droits*	stamp duty and fees

Wertschriften Ti-tel	*titres*	securities
Depot	*depot*	safe custody
Abschluss per	*arrêté au*	closed per
Betrag	*montant*	amount
1. Soll-Zinssatz	*ler taux int. debi-teur*	1st debit int. rate
Limite fur 1.Soll-Zins	*Limite pour ler taux deb*	Limit of 1st debit int. rate
Soll-Zinssatz	*2me taux int. debiteur*	2nd debit int. rate
Haben-Zinssatz	*Taux int. crean-cier*	Credit int. rate
Komm.a.Soll-Umsatz	*Comm s.mut. debiteur*	Commission on debit turnover
Komm.vom hochsten Soll Saldo	*Comm s.le.solde deb.Maximum*	Commission on highest balance
Kreditlimite	Limite de credit	Limit of credit
Saldo zu Irhen Lasten	*Solde en notre fa-veur*	Balance in our fa-vor
Abschluss erfolgt auf separatem blatt	*Bouclement voir page separe*	Status see sepa-rate page

Frankoposten	*Mouvement franco*	free of commission
Abschlussbuch-ung	*Ecriture de bou-clement*	summary of closing
Bemerkungen	*Observations*	Remarks
Buchungen nach dem	*Les operations effectuees*	Entries after closing date
Abschlussdatum erscheinen	*apres la date de cloture*	appear on new statement
in neuer Rech-nung	*apparaitront sur le prochain*	
Geldwechsel	*Change*	Exchange
Reisechecks	*Cheques de voy-age*	Travelers Checks
Benzincoupons	*Bons d'essence*	Petrol coupons
Samtliche Bank-geschafte	*Toutes opera-tions bancaires*	All banking transactions
Deckung	*Garantie*	Collateral
Zinsen	*interets*	interest
./.,minus,weniger	*moins*	less
Nettobetrag, zu Ihren Gunsten	*produit net en votre faveur*	net proceeds in your favor
Spesen	*frais*	charges, expenses

Deckungskom-		
mission	*commission de*	
	couverture	cover commission
Portospesen	*frais de ports*	postage
Zum Kurse von	*au cours de*	at the rate of
ergebend	*produisant*	producing
Tage	*jours*	days
Konto	*compte*	account
Betrag und		
Zinsen	*montant et inter-*	
	ets	principal plus interest
Fr.	*frs*	Swiss francs
DM	*DM*	German marks
Lit.	*Lit.*	Italian lire
Sch.	*Sch.*	Austrian schilling
Frb.	*frb.*	Belgian francs
Hfl.	*fl.*	Dutch florin
Ptas.	*ptas.*	Spanish pesetas
Skr.	*cr.s.*	Swedish crowns
Dkr.	*cr.d.*	Danish crowns
Nkr.	*cr.n.*	Norwegian crowns
FMk	*markka*	Finnish marks

Be prepared for your bank's *name* to appear quite different from what you thought it was. It may give you a form with the name in Italian one day, French the next, German the next and you may lose track of whom you are doing business with. Example: People's Bank of Switzerland comes out as Schweiserische Volksbank in German and as Banque Populaire Suisse in French.

Also, outside the US no country believes in speed for the sake of speed. So the rate at which things are done may frustrate you. The threat of "I will take my business elsewhere," which can dramatically speed up any desired action in the States, will have virtually no effect here. They may even urge you to go elsewhere. Also you will get little or no sales talk. Generally the banker will discuss various investment possibilities with you as if he were bored with the whole subject. He lacks what Americans would call "flair." But this is not a bad thing, and the lack of so-called flair has enabled the Swiss banks to weather untold storms. They neither get highly enthusiastic about things, nor do they readily withdraw when things look gloomy. No banners, no P.R., no piped music, just unimaginative, solid and sound banking practice.

You will also find that you can arrive at some foreign banks with money to deposit and they just may not take it. They will want to take your references first. This does not always apply in Switzerland but it's very common in England where they usually won't even take your money *pending* references. And *cash* is often looked upon as less desirable than checks. If you are not well referred you can keep your money.

However, the whole reason for going abroad is to obtain a stability temporarily lacking at home, and so one has to learn to live with and accommodate to those things that *enable* that stability to exist. Stability has never been an attractive quality, but it is a very *comfortable* quality, particularly when things are increasingly unstable all around.

PART 5

*Timing and Outlook
(the "When" Factor)*

CHAPTER 15

How Long Must I Invest Abroad?

"For my part, I travel not to go anywhere, but to go. I travel for travel's sake. The great affair is to move." Robert Louis Stevenson

HOPEFULLY this book has laid the groundwork for you to think more internationally as far as investments are concerned. Soon moving your money from country to country, depending on the political and economic position at any given time, will become as easy as moving from one industry group to another within the US stock market.

But whether you decide to bring your money back to the US or whether you decide to "move it on," there are some general rules for such a movement which I will attempt to elaborate here.

When to Move Your Money Back to the USA

The instability of the present monetary system disrupts trade and interferes with living standards. We need a system that restricts governments' abilities to inflate and does not allow them to point accusing fingers at other people when they (the governments) get into trouble. Such a system would encourage trade and investment from abroad because it would stimulate confidence in the government and hope in the future. At the moment we have a monetary system wherein the two major currencies forming the greater part of world reserves are very weak, making the whole international monetary complex suspect. The self-correcting mechanism no longer works, and so everybody (even those with relatively strong currencies) is attempting to hold the system together for a little bit longer and a little bit longer.

How long they will manage to hold the system so together is impossible to predict. As you will have seen in the earlier chapters of this book, once things are going really wrong, it is merely a battle between government and confidence. In most cases governments can hold up confidence long *after* the disappearance of any reason for there to *be* any confidence. Historically few governments have ever taken the proper action voluntarily. Usually they do the right thing only when there is no other alternative, and they invariably call the right thing "the lesser of evils."

Unless the current governments in the world prove to be infinitely more enlightened than their predecessors throughout history, the pattern will be more loans and swaps to one another, more taxation, more blaming of the public for the sins of government, more controls, and then more of the same, until ultimately when nothing works, the system is declared null and void and restructured (i.e. revaluation or devaluation, inflation curbs, etc.).

Therefore while the "system," as it is, continues to function, albeit more inefficiently as months go by, then there is nothing one can do but wait. Throughout this period of waiting there will be moments of doubt as to whether one's basic premises are correct, or whether there is indeed anything wrong with the system. In order to answer this, one should ask oneself the following: Are taxes being cut? Are wages no longer rising? Are prices staying level? Or falling? Does real prosperity abound? Are governments no longer trying to sell the public on the system and now keeping quiet and just going about their business? Is there some new backing for money that is self-regulatory? If the answer is no to these questions then nothing has changed, and it is merely the timing that is depressing.

Hence one should wait for the following changes before bringing back funds:

1. Either a revaluation of gold, or a devaluation of the dollar or a period of prolonged and painful credit squeeze which would have brought the dollar back to a point where 35 paper dollars really are worth one ounce of gold and US prices are again competitive.

2. Period of readjustment on the economic scene, whereby prices are not rising, and neither are wages. Actual price *cuts* should be occasionally seen.

3. General feeling of world confidence in USA economic and fiscal policy, and in US politics generally.

4. Technical signs in the stock market to indicate that a new Bull Market has begun, probably following a period of low volume, low prices, and general disinterest.

5. The willingness of a man to do a dollar's worth of work for a dollar paid.

6. Gradual lessening of controls rather than increasing.

7. Talk of tax cuts rather than increases.

8. General low morale at home whereby people feel things will never be as good again (when they believe this it's usually at the turn; "Buy when the blood is running in the streets," as Rothschild said).

9. Every indication that the US dollar is back on an historically stable standard, such as gold, whereby it is *self-regulating* rather than *politically* regulating. Ideally this would include dollar redeemability also. When most of these signs are evident, particularly the dollar being devalued or gold revalued, then one should get out of Swiss Francs or whatever "sound" currency one is in, VERY fast. The reason for this is that the presently sound currencies will suffer from other people feeling the dollar is again sound and money will flow out. Therefore the Swiss Franc and other such hard currencies would likely devalue very

soon after the US dollar did so. The trick will be to get back into dollars before that happens and so avoid being caught with a foreign devaluation after having profited from a US devaluation. Do nothing unless devaluation is substantial.

Closing Your Account Abroad

Closing a bank account abroad is no more difficult than closing one at home; neither is bringing the money back. It can be expedited in ways similar to those you used to put it there in the first place. Provided you have stayed in good companies in the purchase of stock then there is no problem disposing of foreign stock at quoted prices. However, certain types of bonds and long-term depository notes and fixed deposits and bank accounts require a predetermined amount of notice before they can be liquidated or withdrawn. It is well to establish what this is when you buy or open them, and also to establish what the penalty is for cutting short the period agreed upon.

The Advantages of Keeping Part of Assets Abroad Permanently

1. If you travel to any extent then to have a Swiss or other foreign account is an advantage. Your Swiss banker can be used as reference in many countries and as an *entré* to contacts you might wish to make.
2. By keeping an account permanently in Switzerland, or some other international market place, you continue to keep that international outlook and maneuverability. If you wish to "trade interest rates" from country to country, you'll find trying to do this from the USA without accounts abroad is almost impossible for the private citizen.
3. Diversification is always a good idea regardless of how things look at home. As soon as you bring the money "home" you are back to a *one-country* concept.
4. The leverage that can be achieved abroad is better than

can be achieved at home (i.e. lower margin, possibility of using one investment as security against another which cannot be done either at all or as far in the USA).

5. By keeping a source abroad it can be used for paying for holidays abroad, educating the children abroad, making business deals, etc. One can often make money merely by seeing that one's money is transferred from one currency to another, when the rate is favorable, and then leaving it there, rather than just exchanging it as needed.

6. As this is written the growth rate in the Common Market and in Japan and in Australia is higher than in the US. So to bring home all one's investment capital after a US devaluation would prevent you from participating in markets where there is currently more potential. You can maximize profits by shifting to the most-growing country, and it can all be done without ever leaving your Swiss bank.

CHAPTER 16

Conclusions and Predictions

"I shall always consider the best guesser the best prophet."
Cicero

WHILE Cicero oversimplified the problem of prophecy, there is certainly some truth in what he said. The ability to predict is probably the ability to weigh, more carefully than most, the facts on hand and to define the trend, or change in trend, or special event. There is no supernatural aspect. Anyhow, I am entitled to some guesses as much as the next man. So what follows is, I trust, a logical guess of what will happen over the next decade.

The biggest problem when predicting future events is putting a time scale on them. Those who see, through logic, what is to come invariably underestimate the stupidity and/or gullibility of mankind and thus underestimate the period of time between the moment things start going wrong and the moment the public starts getting frightened (when they too have realized things are going wrong).

The most famous example of this perhaps was Roger Babson in 1926 who predicted a crash that didn't arrive till 1929. He was right, merely early, but how he must have been ridiculed for those three years. Also, Winston Churchill predicted war with Germany early in the 30's but it was a long time coming. The wheels of political and economic negotiation move slowly.

Wall Street has technically been in a Bear Market since January 1966. This assertion is based on: a) continuous downtrending of the advance-decline line (which reflects all shares listed) and which has repeatedly gone to new lows; b) daily new highs gradually weakening over recent years, showing a minority of stocks able to go to new highs (even for the year, let alone all-time), while new lows have swollen on each wave, for example running to over 700 in a day, in mid-1970; c) Dow Theory, widely misunderstood and misapplied but almost unfailing under proper interpretation; d) Dow Jones Industrial Average has failed to exceed its '66 peak and failed to confirm any speculative average, including transportation, glamour, low-priced American Stock Exchange; e) every major monetary yardstick is and has been increasingly bearish for four years. Stock markets can't thrive in a climate of no-confidence-currency, credit-crunch, high interest, escalating inflation. My contention has been, for four years, that we have been in a *monetary* bear market, rather than a business bear market. I would extend this to say: even if inflation somehow swept market averages up, if people stampeded out of cash into shares, we would still be in a monetary bear market and no real and true prosperity would exist, nor would such a stock market be sound or safe, for prices would be relatively unrelated to earnings. Price-earnings ratios might increase, but this would hardly be healthy. Not until the monetary mess is resolved can the monetary bear market begin to phase out. This probably requires one to three years more, give or take a bit (i.e. 1971–1974).

Gold was revalued last time just over four years after the 1929 top. If we assume there was some cause-and-effect reason for that size of time lag, and if it is repeated on a two-to-one time scale basis (as prosperity has when compared to the 1920's prosperity), then the revaluation date would be 1973. Assuming gold will be revalued to $60-$70, then based on the current rate of rise gold will have hit $60 on the so-called free market by 1971 or thereabouts. Gold *shares* should begin anticipating this in 1970.

Last time gold was revalued, and the dollar was thus de facto devalued, there was a deflationary depression first. Must this happen again? Not necessarily. There was a depression last time partly because Mr. Hoover had a policy of allowing prices and wages to adjust *down* to hard money (instead of bringing hard money, i.e. gold, *up* to prices and wages). He let the country adjust itself in the free market. This policy won't sell any more. He was trying what Churchill simultaneously was trying to do, i.e. bring back an economy to a *pre-W.W.I* price of gold. People didn't like it and elected Roosevelt, who had other ideas. His tack was the opposite—i.e. when the debtor is in trouble, eradicate the debt and begin going into debt all over again, instead of paying it off as Hoover did.

Because so much "social legislation" has been built into the law, Mr. Nixon has less room to maneuver than either Mr. Hoover or FDR. Based on this and current-day social trends (i.e. the growing acceptance that government is obligated to "create" permanent prosperity) I would think that gold revaluation (and dollar devaluation) may come at a point when America appears to be headed into a serious depression. By this I do not mean a planned and enforced recession such as we have had at intervals since 1945. Periodically governments the world over, since World War II, have "squeezed" their economies in order to attempt to make the prosperity last a little longer. Based on the past record, an adjustment in stock market terms of around 40-45% is easily possible (i.e. DJI 700-750) without hurting a long-term uptrend which began in the 1800's.

The problem is, however, much like a car going at increasing speed. As you drive along at 30 mph, you find the speed gradually increases to 40 mph. This you decide a bit unsafe so you apply brake pressure until it is back to, say,

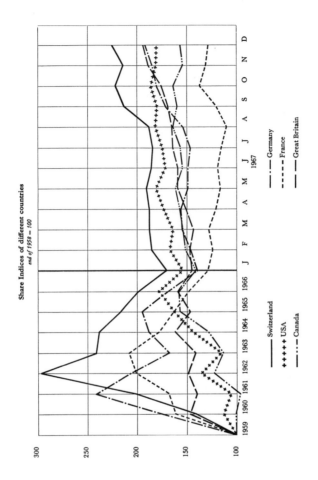

This chart was selected precisely because it is *not* current, thus
enabling a dispassionate view of a 9-year period of recent history that is separated from today's markets in time. It illustrates
how poor was the performance of the US stock market for the
first five years shown, and how Switzerland has given the best
performance of the countries shown.

35 mph. A little later you notice the speed has crept up to 50 mph and you apply pressure and get back to 40 mph, and so on until when you try to brake at, say, 120 mph you go into a skid and can't control it. This is rather like what happens to an economy. At each juncture where the government feels that a certain squeeze is necessary in order to maintain long-term prosperity, it only brakes a certain amount. The population of a country with a democratic government will only accept a limited amount of backtracking. For example a man might reluctantly swallow certain increases in prices but he (or his union) would refuse to take a cut in wages. He might accept a wage freeze while prices rise, say, 5% in a year. But more than this governments CANNOT do and stay popular. So the amount of squeeze they apply is *invariably* slightly *less* than is really required. Hence the fact that the economy gets "hotter" as time goes by.

There comes a point, however, in the inflationary cycle when trying to "squeeze" makes the whole thing get out of hand, and this beautiful "stop-go" mechanism that had worked at slower speeds may no longer work, either because it creates a string of chain reaction, making it impossible to lift the squeeze once it has been applied, or because rampant inflation sets in, which may fool everybody with sheer numbers for a while, but still amounts in real value to loss of purchasing power and slump. At the time of this writing the US economy is sitting more or less at the juncture between recession and rampant inflation. The stock market too is near that 25% mark. And so we wait with bated breath to see if the government is really still in control and can lift things for yet another few months/years of unbacked, unsupported prosperity.

One must also reckon with emotion. Once a depression and/or market-crash *psychology* grips the mass mind

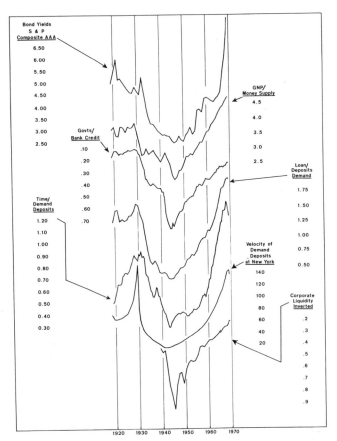

An indication of the severity of US monetary conditions in 1970 (which cannot be corrected overnight) is seen in this chart showing various key elements. Excessive money supply is evident, as are historic yields. Corporate liquidity is perilous. Among the most ominous indicators is velocity of demand deposits at New York, showing a peak almost identical with 1929. Collectively, they say the U.S. is in a monetary bear market and a major change of direction is necessary to save the situation. An increase in the gold price is one of the corrective ingredients, but is not of itself sufficient. Certain deflationary measures are necessary as well.

(Chart courtesy: Bank Credit Analyst, 1245 Sherbrooke St. West, Montreal, and Monetary Research Ltd., P.O. Box 498, Hamilton, Bermuda) (which is traditional every so often) the mood would gain momentum and "could" carry the DJIA well below 700, to 500 or even lower. This is logic-projection, not strictly forecasting. One should therefore plan with this grim possibility in mind, however remote it may seem to be.

In other areas things *are* pointing to "loss of control" (by government) and so it would seem a fair guess that in the field of economics government is also losing control. Socially government has failed:

1. to alleviate poverty, in spite of the vast sums of tax money spent.

2. to combat crime, which is on the increase to the point of making the formation of private vigilante groups necessary.

3. to control schools. America is, unless things change, producing a generation of Americans that will be probably the most illiterate since the early colonial days.

I am sure you can add other areas where it is obvious that there is a loss of control, not the least of course is the Vietnam war. And the race "war." Hence it would seem unrealistic to imagine that in the field of economics there should be an exception and that government is totally in control. And in order to make the government "stop-go" intervention work, IT MUST BE IN TOTAL CONTROL.

The next few months will be the crucial test. From the guidelines in this book you will be able to predict the natural result yourself.

If America does go off into a skid economically, then the US government will possibly feel that in order to attempt to stop it, devaluation would be the least of evils. However, it may try other things first, such as wage freezes, price control, greater capital outflow control, even some new form of exchange control. Obviously if such controls may be inflicted, it is well for investors to have acted *before* rather than *after* these are enforced. Capital preservation is becoming increasingly difficult.

Attempting to put a *time* stamp on this series of events is like trying to bet how many minutes the drunk will remain conscious after it is obvious he is drunk. There just isn't any rule, because you are betting against people's reactions, not merely predicting trends in a free-market place.

What is more realistic is to recognize the beginning of a chain of events and know that when such and such happen then this, this and this will follow within a period of months to several years.

When the government has finally decided that devaluation is the least of evils, then, although this will not create an instant miracle, it will lay the basis for a later recovery. Prices could drift off in a multi-year erosion rather than a 1929-style crash, prior to the turn. Much depends on what measures are introduced along with a devaluation.

I have referred only vaguely to the possibility of runaway inflation, and of government inflating its way out of debt. More specifically let me say that although a true runaway inflation (i.e. upwards of 30% a year) is not an odds-on favorite, it has at *least* a 1-in-4 chance of coming to pass. The implications here are manifold and space doesn't allow a full exposition of possibilities. But among them are these: the world splitting into a dollar-bloc and a gold-bloc, dollar devaluation by *other* nations, economic chaos and ultimate depression of the worst sort, civil war fostered by the disproportionate burden borne by blacks in the US in economic squeeze, gold repricing first by Europe and ultimately by the US to well over $100 an ounce, and at its worst runaway inflation could yield a substitution of one new "hard" dollar for two (or more) old dollars. Inflation out of hand is the worst of all worlds so the negative aspects are almost limitless, as in the German inflation of the 1920's. Again I don't list these as my forecasts, per se, but rather as what could result if the longshot (hyper-inflation) should gain control. What is now more likely is chronic inflation of 15-20% a year with stagnating business profits and a dull stock market that does not keep pace with currency debasement. Neither US shares nor dollars would be prudent to hold. This too leads to devaluation, perhaps a series of minor ones.

To paraphrase: it's unlikely that modern-day politicians will watch the market fall 95% (as in 1929–32) and have banks close, and unemployment mount, without trying every mirror trick in the bag, and repricing gold would be seen by them as one of those tricks. After this has been done, then presumably America will go through the per-formance of "making devaluation work" as Britain did in 1968 and 1969, which would mean continuing controls and a permanent threat of a second devaluation. Hence it is well to wait for the first lessening of controls before one assumes the worst is over.

When It Is All Over

Assuming we are at that point when one believes that it is indeed all over, what then? Bonds would be a reasonable investment for the conservative-minded. Blue chip stock sitting at low prices will be bargains, and probably the first to benefit from a new prosperity. This would also be a time to buy property. Perhaps antiques, art, and such will be worth considering. It would be the time to get out of francs and into assets. Just which industry groups will be best then depends on many things, such as the outcome of the Vietnam war, which industries if any government is offer-ing big contracts to, how the world has progressed. For example, who knows, the "home computer industry" may be *the* industry then. A computer in every home is a likelihood.

But whatever the current craze, the same basic investment policies will apply then as *any* time. That is, you should not overextend yourself, you should diversify, and you should not aim at "killings" (for those who look for a killing usually find it, and get killed themselves). It is much better to hope that your money will work for you conservatively over a period of years than to hope that you will be able to double your money in three or six months in some hot-shot issue. While you should of course constantly monitor your investments, the need to drastically *change* them should arise very seldom if you make the right decisions in the first place, and hopefully, when the international monetary muddle is sorted out, we shall be able to sit back for the ensuing decade and watch things grow, perhaps slowly at first, but in any event at least consistently, and on a firmer foundation.

Appendix

US Laws on Foreign Accounts

THERE have frequently been controversial proposals made over the years in the US to restrict Americans' foreign bank accounts, or to force citizens to give information about them, etc. The pretexts and reasons vary with the times and politicians and balance of payments. But whether it is the US or any other country, past and current history is overflowing with examples which conclusively prove that the more legislation a government introduces to contain and control money, the more money runs out of the country.

It is also axiomatic that ways are found *around* every law—and especially so in regard to money. Thus, whether or not any new legislation is passed in the US requiring US citizens to declare where they have money abroad, it will be of no benefit to the country and will not succeed in thwarting enterprising citizens who rightly grow increasingly wary of a government that restricts their freedom to do what they will with their money. The US will find other nations will retaliate against any such laws, however mild, and should they not be mild, the retaliation would be extensive indeed.

Nor will many US citizens be long deterred by new rules that may come to pass. Some will place funds abroad and refuse to report it. That's human nature. Others will report it freely—feeling that money is safer elsewhere and the government rules only tend to prove it. I would not let the rules disturb me. Working *within* the laws now proposed allows ample latitude to place funds. Should much more strict laws be passed (which I deem unlikely for reasons stated above), I predict they would be short-lived. Bad laws don't usually last long. Nor do unenforceable laws. When you have a combination of bad *and* unenforceable laws, it is rare they are on the books for long.

If, at any time in the future, excessive pressure is put on Swiss banks by US authorities, and if the Swiss give too much ground for the comfort of their worldwide depositors, those depositors will begin to move all or a portion of their funds into other countries—like Canada (especially Quebec), Sweden, South Africa, Germany, Holland, Australia, Lebanon, Mexico, France, Luxembourg, England, South Ireland, or the small island tax havens, etc., diversifying between several of them and altering arrangements as fits the changing laws and pressures. Most of these countries provide bank secrecy in varying degrees. I say this as a warning to the Swiss government not to let any of her sovereignty or independence be pried away from her (even though I doubt my warning is needed), and I say it to give comfort to those who seek havens—for there will *always* emerge a haven for money seeking safety and privacy. It has ever been thus.

However, do not let me frighten you. Americans are "gun-shy" since they live in a country where government bureaus are often given frightening power, especially the IRS and CIA and FCC and SEC. Such fear may be justified in the USA, but it isn't justified in most of the rest of the Free World. The Swiss will not, in my opinion, cooperate with foreign tax authorities except in the most *extreme* criminal cases—regardless of any impression that may be given for the sake of good public relations. This is because tax offenses are not criminal in Switzerland and because banking is her main business and because she has a proud tradition of independence and because the Swiss abhor government interference—their own or anyone else's.

Take with a grain of salt any announcement made by US authorities about agreements with the Swiss over exchange of information. The Swiss will, in practice, only help where a man is a high Mafia boss or has removed the entire contents of Fort Knox's vaults. The US should neither ask nor expect any more from a foreign and sovereign nation.

Harassment

I doubt that the possession of a foreign bank account will be declared to be illegal for Americans, at least so far as we can see now, which admittedly is only 1–2 years ahead. But currency controls could well increase and might easily limit the *amount* you could send abroad. All this augurs in favor of making any contemplated deposits of this sort sooner rather than later. But even without new controls you can be fairly well assured that foreign accounts will be discouraged, either through harassment or the main US government tactic: intimidation. US laws are not, generally, uniformly enforced; most citizens are merely intimidated. Fear tactics have long since taken over for equal justice-for-all, known in the days of the Founding Fathers and the inception of the Constitution. At minimum, look for the usual haranguing by bureaucrats, who will imply that such accounts are unethical or unpatriotic. In fact, they will be saying that they don't want you to remain solvent if the government and nation are insolvent. They don't realize that only solvent citizens can provide capital to rebuild the economy amidst the ashes of a financial fiasco.

To most government people, anything they don't control is unethical. It is primarily the tax-collecting agency that feels this way, although the agency tries to imply that it is the entire government for which it speaks.

On a practical level, the most that can be anticipated at this stage by way of direct action is an attempt to coerce citizens to incriminate themselves—a clear violation of the Fifth Amendment of the US Constitution. Indeed, *signing* an income tax form is already thought by many to be unconstitutional and some are refusing to do so, on these self-incrimination grounds. Even so, the US Treasury is hoping to get legislation to include a question on the US income tax form asking whether you have a foreign bank account. Again, intimidation is the automatic form US bureaucracy and legislation take these days in place of a straightforward black or white stand—that foreign accounts are either legal or illegal. If they are legal then the question has no place on the form. It is asking you: are you doing something which is legal? It is tyrant talk. The increased use of intimidation by government is always a sign, historically, that a country is degenerating. It should also help you decide whether or not the time has come for you to take steps to build your ark. In Noah's terms, it has already started to rain.

Letters to Switzerland

In November-December 1969 there was some admitted spotchecking of Swiss-bound mail from the USA by tax men to determine the amount of the postal flow to Swiss banks. Details of the spying were not revealed but obviously no letters were opened. It was apparently a head-count of envelopes. The purpose was evidently to provide testimony for proposed legislation to force Americans to report the existence of foreign accounts. Whether such spotchecking will occur again or whether any record was or will ever be kept is impossible to say, but the labor required to do so would be massive and virtually impossible to monitor with accuracy. Further, it is unlikely to be again needed, for legislation. Obviously if complete censorship of mail (opening, etc.) should ever take place, the US would no longer be a free country in even the remotest sense, and a mass exodus of monied people would follow. This book presumes such a total transition to dictatorship or state control will not take place, or at least not in the near term—which is probably all one can hope to plan for with accuracy.

Some citizens, Americans or other, wish *complete* (100%) privacy for their bank accounts and for their mail, even though they are breaking no laws. They achieve this in various ways, for example by sending mail to their foreign banks *by way of* friends or via accommodation bureaus in a third country (e.g. Canada, England, France, and almost anywhere). Likewise they provide for *return* mail from those banks by the same route. In this way no mail goes directly to or comes directly from the country where they bank. Alternatively many (especially Europeans) ask the bank to mail nothing, to *hold* all mail, which controls their incoming mail. Outgoing mail is frankly a highly unlikely cause for privacy infringement in any country outside the Iron Curtain.

Mail censorship is, to my knowledge and except during a declared and major war, illegal, and unconstitutional in all countries of the West. So aside from the fact that the staff required to do so would be unwieldy and an unmerited expense, the repugnance of such an odious act would cause a mass protest that would end the practice if ever begun in the US. Thus I personally doubt anything more than spotchecking of envelopes (to ascertain bulk flow) will ever be done in the US—at least in the foreseeable future under the present form of government.

Swiss Banks Abroad

As an example of how extensive are the branches of some Swiss banks, here is a list of only the foreign offices of Swiss Bank Corporation, whose headquarters is in Basel. By the way, its end of year statement for 1969 showed assets of 22,085,567,239 Swiss Francs.

NEW YORK BRANCH
Main Office: 15 Nassau Street, New York, N.Y. 10005
Swiss Center Office, 608 Fifth Avenue, New York, N.Y. 10020

SAN FRANCISCO AGENCY
120 Montgomery St., San Francisco, Cal. 94104

LONDON OFFICES
99 Gresham St., E.C.2, and 1 New Coventry St., W.1

AFFILIATES
Canada: Swiss Corporation for Canadian Investments Ltd., 800 Dorchester Blvd.West, Suite 1620, Montreal 101
Swiss Corporation for Canadian Investments Ltd., 25 King Street West, Suite 1330, Toronto 1
Morocco: Banque Americano-Franco-Suisse pour le Maroc, 26 Avenue de l'Armee Royale, Casablanca
Bahamas: Swiss Bank Corporation (Overseas) Limited, Carib House, George Street, P.O. Box 757, Nassau
Panama: Swiss Bank Corporation (Overseas) Limited, Edificio Avesa, Via Espana, Apartado 61, Panama 9A

REPRESENTATIVE OFFICES
Los Angeles: Suite 532, 510 West Sixth Street, Los Angeles, Cal. 90014

Lebanon: Beirut Riyad Bldg., Riad Solh Street, Boite Post-
ale 6059, Beirut
Argentina: Reconquista 458, Buenos Aires
Hong Kong: 1604 Hang Chong Building, 5 Queen's Road
Central
South Africa: Swiss House, 86 Main Street, P. O. Box
8549, Johannesburg
Peru: Camana 370-Of. 703, Casilla 1289, Lima
Spain: Alcala 95-6, Madrid 9
Mexico: Torre Latinoamericana, San Juan de Letran,
2-3203, Mexico 1, D.F. Apartado Postal M-2872
France: 31 Avenue de l'Opera, Paris 1er
Brazil: Avenida Rio Branco 99, 18.andar, Caixa postal
1446-ZC-00, Rio de Janeiro
Rua libero Badaro 293 (conj.29A), Caixa postal 30.485,
Sao Paulo
Australia: Australia Square Building (Suite 4216), Box
2690 G.P.O., Sydney, NSW 2001
Japan: Kokusai Building (Suite 920), Marunouchi, Chiyo-
da-Ku, P.O. Box Central 513, Tokyo

A list of banks in various European countries may be of
value to some readers. Space wouldn't permit a complete
listing so this will be a compilation only of key cities and
of only the US banks plus two major local banks. It will not
include Switzerland since its banks have been covered in
the main body of the book. Bank hours are included.

ANDORRA (Andorra La Vella) Mon-Fri 9.00-13.00; 15.-
00-17.30. Sat 9.00-12.00
Banc Agricol i Comercial, 3 Placa Princep Benlloch
Crédit Andorra, 19 Princep Benlloch

AUSTRIA (Vienna) Mon-Fri 8.00-15.30 (Fri to 17.30)
American Express Intl. Bkg., 21 Kärntnerstrasse

Bank of America, 13 Rotenturmstrasse
Genossenschaftliche Zentralbank, 1 Herrengasse
Oesterreischische Länderbank, 2 Am Hof

BELGIUM (Brussels) Mon-Fri 9.00-1300; 15.00-16.00
American Express Intl. Bkg., 22 Place Rogier
Bank of America, 1 Place Madou
Banque of Bruxelles, 2 Rue de la Régence
Banque Nationale de Belgique, 5 Bd. de Berlaimont
Chase Manhattan Overseas, 51 Av. des Arts
Contnl. Illinois Natl. Bank, 19 R. Chancellerie
Crocker-Citizens National Bank. 5 R. de Loxum
First Nat. Bank of Chicago, 40 Av. des Arts
First National City Bank, 8 Rue Cardinal Mercier
Manufacturers Hanover Trust, 52 R. des Colonies
Morgan Guaranty Trust Co., 27 Av. des Arts

CYPRUS (Nicosia) Mon-Fri 8.30-12.00
Bank of Cyprus, 86 Phaneromeni Street
Central Bank of Cyprus, 38 Metohiou Avenue

DENMARK (Copenhagen) Mon-Fri 9.30-15.00 (Tue &
Fri 16.30-18.00)
Bank of America, 40 Norregade
Den Danske Landmandsbank, 12 Holmens Kanal
Privatabanken i Kjobenhavn, 4 Borsgade

ENGLAND (London) Mon-Fri 9.30-15.30
American Express Intl. Bkg., 25 Abchurch Lane
American Nat. Bk. & Tr. Chicago, 24 Austin Friars
Bank of America, 27 Walbrook
Bank of New York, 147 Leadenhall Street
Bankers Trust Company, 9 Queen Victoria Street
Barclays D.C.O. 33 Old Broad Street

Chase Manhattan, Woolgate House, Coleman Street
Chemical Bank, 10 Moorgate
City Natl. Bank of Detroit, 52 Cornhill
Continental Illinois Natl. Bank, 58 Moorgate
Crocker-Citizens National Bank, 34 Gt. St. Helens
Detroit Bank & Trust, P. & O. Bldg, Leadenhall
First National Bank of Boston, 4 Moorgate
First Natl. Bk. of Chicago, 1 Royal Exchange Buildings
First National City Bank, 34 Moorgate
First Pennsylvania Bkg. & Trust, 38 Walbrook
First Wisconsin National Bank, 39 New Broad Street
Franklin National Bank, 27 Old Jewry
Lloyds Bank, Head Office, 71 Lombard Street
Manufacturers Hanover Turst, 88 Brook Street, W.1
Marine Midland Grace Trust, 5 Lothbury
Mellon National Bank & Trust, 13 Moorgate
Morgan Guaranty Trust Co., 33 Lombard Street
National Bank of Detroit, 28 King Street
Security Pacific Natl. Bk., 18 Finsbury Circus
United California Bank, 35 Moorgate
Wells Fargo Bank, 1 Broad St. Place
Western American Bank, 18 Finsbury Circus

FINLAND (Helsinki) Mon-Fri 9.00-18.00
Bank of Finland, 8 Snellmaninkatu
Helsingfors Aktiebank, 17 Aleksanterinkatu

FRANCE (Paris) Mon-Fri 9.00-12.00; 14.00-16.00
American Express INTL. Bkg., 11 Rue Scribe
Bank of America (Intl.), 28 Place Vendôme
Bankers Trust Company, 2 Av. Montaigne
Banque de France, 39 Rue Croix-Petits-Champs
Chase Manhattan Bank, 41 Rue Cambon
Chemical Bank, 12 Pl. Vendôme

Continental Illinois Natl. Bk., 10 Av. Montaigne
First National Bank of Boston, 21 Pl. Vendôme
Irving Trust Company, 9 Rue Tronchet
Manufacturers Hanover Trust, 20 Pl. Vendôme
Marine Midland Grace, 21 Pl. Vendôme
Morgan Guaranty Trust Co., 14 Place Vendôme
Pittsburgh National Bank, 20 Place Vendôme
Société Générale, 29 Boulevard Haussmann

GERMANY (Frankfurt am Main) Mon-Fri 8.30-13.00;
14.30-16.00 (Fri 16.00-18.00)
Allgemeine Bankgesellschaft, 52 Bockenh'mr Anlage
American Express Bank, 13 Bockenheimer Lanstr.
Bank of America, 9 Savignystrasse
Bankers Trust Company, 3 Goetheplatz
Chase Manhattan Bank, 24 Bockenheimer Landstr.
Chemical Bank, 2 Bockenheimer Landstr.
Crocker-Citizens National Bank, 21 Taunusanlage
Deutsche Bank, 5 Junghofstrasse-Rossmarkt
Exchange Nat. Bank of Chicago, 31 Neue Mainzerstr.
First National City Bank, 16 Grosse Gallusstrasse
Manufacturers Hanover Trust, 51 Bockenheimer Landstr.
Marine Midland Grace, 65 Bockenheimer Landstr.
Morgan Guaranty Trust Co., Zürich-Hochhaus

GREECE (Athens) Mon-Sat 8.00-13.00
American Express Intl. Bkg., Constitution Square
Bank of America, 10 Stadiou Street
Bank of Greece, 21 El. Venizelou Avenue
Chase Manhattan Bank, 2 Vas. Sophias Avenue
Commercial Bank of Greece, 11 Sophocles St.
First National City Bank, 8 Othonos Street

ITALY (Rome)
Winter: Mon-Fri 8.30-12.30; 15.30-16.45
Summer: Mon-Fri 8.30-12.30; 15.45-17.00
American Express Bank, 5 Piazza Mignanelli
Banca Commerciale Italiana, 226 Via del Corso
Bance d' America e d'Italia, 161 Largo Tritone
Bankers Trust Company, 76 Via Bissolati
Chase Manhattan Bank, 57 Via Bissolati
Credito Italiano, 374 Via del Corso
First National City Bank, 26 Via Boncompagni
Manufacturers Hanover Trust, 76 Via Bissolati
Morgan Guaranty Trust Company, 11 Via Parigi

LIECHTENSTEIN (Vaduz) Mon-Fri 8.00-12.00; 14.00-
17.00
Bank in Liechtenstein AG
Liechtensteinische Landesbank

LUXEMBOURG (Luxembourg) Mon-Fri 8.30-12.00;
14.00-17.00
Bank of America, 8 Boulevard Royal
Banque Lambert-Luxembourg, 59 Boulevard Royal
Cie Luxembourgeoise de Banque, 34a R. Philippe II
Wells Fargo Bank, 2 Rue Heine

NETHERLANDS (Amsterdam) Mon-Fri 9.00-15.00
American Express Intl. Bkg., 66 Damrak
Amsterdam-Rotterdam Bank, 595 Herengracht
Bank of America, 237 Herengracht
First National City Bank, 545 Herengracht
Nederlandsche Bank, Frederiksplein

NORTHERN IRELAND (Belfast) Mon-Thur 10.00-12.-
30; 13.30-15.30. Fri 9.30-12.30; 13.30-17.00

National Bank of Ireland, 62 High Street
Ulster Bank, 35 Waring Street

NORWAY (Oslo) Mon-Fri 8.45-16.15 (Thur to 18.00)
Den norske Creditbank, 21 Kirkegaten
Landsbanken, 11 Youngsgaten

PORTUGAL (Lisbon) Mon-Fri 9.30-12.00; 14.00-16.00
Sat 9.30-11.30
Banco de Portugal, 148 Rua do Comércio
Banco Português do Atlântico, 112 Rua do Ouro

SCOTLAND (Edinburgh) Mon-Fri 9.30-12.30; 13.30-
15.30 (Thur 16.30-18.30)
Bank of Scotland, The Mound
Royal Bank of Scotland, 42 St. Andrew Square

SPAIN (Madrid) Mon-Sat 9.00-14.00
Banco de Bilbao, 16 Calle de Alcalá
Banco de España, 50 Calle de Alcalá
Bank of America, 3 Marqués de Valdeiglesias
Chase Manhattan Bank, 32 Calle de Alcalá
Cont'l Illinois Nat'l Bank, 48 Av. José Antonio
First National Bank of Boston, 8 Hermosilla
Manufacturers Hanover Trust, 32 Alcalá
Marine Midland Grace, 11 Cedaceros
Morgan Guaranty Trust Company, 8 Barquillo
United California Bank, 10 Cedaceros

SWEDEN (Stockholm) Mon-Fri 9.30-15.00
Svenska Handelsbanken, 11 Arsenalsgatan
Sveriges Kreditbank, 2 Norrmalmstorg

TURKEY (Istanbul) Mon-Fri 9.00-12.30; 14.00-17.00 Sat
9.00-12.00
Amerikan-Türk Dis Tic. Bankasi, 207 Cumhuriyet
Ottoman Bank, 35 Voyvoda Caddesi

Switzerland in a Nutshell

Perhaps the best short summary of the Swiss scene from
a political-financial-historical view ever written is that by
Col. E.C. Harwood, in an April 1969 investment bulletin
for American Institute Counselors, Inc, whose income is
devoted to the support of the American Institute for Economic Research, Great Barrington, Massachusetts 01230.
I think you'll enjoy this piece:

> After prolonged study of all nations in the world that
> merited consideration, we have concluded that Switzer-
> land offers advantages for investment of a portion of one's
> funds and that, for many people, establishment of a legal
> residence in Switzerland offers important tax benefits.
> (U.S. citizenship can be retained even if legal residence in
> Switzerland is established.) The Swiss franc is by far the
> strongest currency in the world, being backed 120 percent
> by gold, compared with the less than 20 percent backing
> of U.S. currency. Moreover, the government of Switzer-
> land is stable, more nearly like that of the United States a
> half century ago than is the present Government of the
> United States itself. If Western civilization declines with
> accompanying social conflict such as that so evident in the
> United States in recent years, we predict that Switzerland
> will endure long after other nations have become commu-
> nist or socialist "welfare states."
>
> In short, if the basic principle of a *limited* central gov-
> ernment and individual freedom are preserved anywhere
> in the world, we believe that they will be in Switzer-
> land.

About Switzerland

There is no country in the world quite like Switzerland. It has succeeded in welding twenty-two states, representing a diversity of European languages and cultures, into one harmonious whole.

Lying in the heart of Europe, Switzerland has a wealth of natural beauty found hardly anywhere else in such a small space. The Alps reach their greatest altitude in Switzerland with the Dufour Peak of Monte Rosa, which is 15,217 feet high. Here is the source of rivers which collect in innumerable valleys and flow to all parts of Europe.

As the land changes from the wild glacier country to the southern mildness of the Rhone valley and the Ticino plain, the conditions of life change too. In the Alps, wooden chalets cling precariously to steep slopes, but the midland farmsteads stand broad and prosperous in their spreading fields.

Liberty, The Essential Feature

Only a free people could attain such a high standard of living and only as a free state could Switzerland, remote from the sea coast and without her own sources of raw materials, command the respect of the whole world and take a prominent part in world trade.

What are the origins of that freedom? Under the Holy Roman Empire, the three communities of Uri, Schwyz and Unterwalden defended themselves against the ambitions of the House of Hapsburg.

The solidarity of the League and the courage of its members were put to severe tests. At Morgarten, in 1315, the Swiss forces crushed the Hapsburg army, and at Sempach, where Winkelried sacrificed his life, they again defeated an army of Austrian knights. In the second half of the 15th century, a threat came from the West, and it was Charles the Bold, Duke of Burgundy, who fell victim of Swiss arms.

After the Treaty of Vienna in 1815, the inner development continued. In 1848, the old federation of states was replaced by the Federal state, which offered all the advantages of a uniform currency and customs duties, a common postal service, a centralized army and a progressive unification of law, civil and penal.

The Nature of the Swiss State

Switzerland is still founded on its member states, the cantons. They are sovereign in so far as their sovereign rights suffer no limitation by the Federal constitution. The Swiss cantons are therefore not mere districts. They resemble the states of the USA but their historical foundation goes much deeper.

In its main features, liberty has been guaranteed for the whole of Switzerland by the Federal constitution. All Swiss citizens are equal before the law, and the constitution expressly abolished all privileges of place, birth, family, or person.

On completion of his twentieth year, every male Swiss becomes an active member of his commune. At the same time he becomes liable for military service in the Swiss militia, which carries on in modern form the tradition of an armed people.

And now we come to *the referendum and the initiative*, the feature of Swiss democracy that has been retained even in the Federal constitution. A bill approved by the Federal Assembly must, under the constitution, be submitted to the referendum. It becomes operative only if no petition is made against it within ninety days.

The people as a whole as well as the cantons are responsible for the election of the legislature, i.e. *the Federal Assembly.* One of the two chambers, the National Council, is representative of the people and is so elected that the 200 seats on the National Council are distributed among the 25 cantons and half-cantons in proportion to population.

The second chamber is elected either by election in the cantons or by the cantonal authorities. It consists of 44 members, inasmuch as each canton has two seats.

The Swiss solution to the problem of executive power within the federal government, on the other hand, is entirely different from the American. In Switzerland the Federal Council heads the executive branch. As a result, the absence of political striving and of a struggle to augment the executive power is noteworthy.

The Federal Council consists of seven members, and they are jointly responsible for the government as a collegial body, while exercising at the same time the functions of head of the state.

The Swiss People

Six and a half centuries of experience have given the Swiss people the most strongly marked national character in Europe. Switzerland with her multiplicity of languages shows clearly that neither language nor race determines the characteristics of a nation.

The Federal Union contained in itself the solution of the minority problem, which is a source of so much difficulty in other countries. In no case does a language group become a majority or a minority with greater or lesser rights, whether in the cantons with three languages such as the Grisons, or with two, such as Berne, Fribourg or Valais.

All this must be kept in mind if the following figures are to be rightly understood. Of the Swiss population, according to the 1960 census, 3,764,000 were German-speaking (693 per 1,000); 1,025,000 French-speaking (189 per 1,000); 51,000 were Romansch-speaking (9 per 1,000) and 75,000 people (14 per 1,000) spoke languages other than these national tongues. All four languages are official languages, and in all of the cities and larger towns English is spoken in most shops and at railway stations or other public places.

A Healthy People

Unceasing efforts are being made to maintain and raise the standard of hygiene in Switzerland. Since the beginning of the century the number of doctors in Switzerland has almost trebled. It is now 7,708, or one practicing doctor for 1,102 inhabitants, while there are also 2,196 dentists.

The urban population constitutes more than a third of the whole, but the urban element is none the less decentralized. Industrialization of Switzerland occurred without the proletarianization of the masses, and nowhere in Switzerland are there the gloomy industrial centers that have sprung up elsewhere. The Swiss worker is not a proletarian, but a civic member of his community by his training and work, by his convictions, and by the esteem in which he is held by his fellow-citizens.

Large estates are entirely unknown in Switzerland. Out of a total of 205,977 farms, as shown by the last trade census in 1955, only 2,489, or not much more than one in eighty, have more than 14 acres of land.

Advantages of Lugano and Vicinity

The vicinity of Lugano and Locarno, the canton of Ticino (Southern Switzerland), has an equable, southern temperate zone climate that is the best available in Europe north of Italy. More hours of sunshine on more days of the year are available here than in most of the European cities such as Paris, Amsterdam, Frankfurt, Zurich, etc.

Except on the mountains above 3,000 feet, snow rarely falls and almost invariably melts the next day. Palm trees are common at the lower elevations. Nevertheless, seasonal changes are sufficient to provide variety without severe heat or cold. Of course, in the mountains, accessible in an hour by car, skiing is available from November to May.

The Ticino climate is widely known in Europe to be beneficial for those who may need or desire a mild climate. Many physicians consider it ideal for heart patients or others who should avoid climatic extremes of prolonged heat or cold.

Living Costs and Tax Savings

The cost of living in Switzerland is roughly one-half to two-thirds that in the United States. Apartment rentals are a little more than half of comparable U.S. rentals. Dining out where one obtains superior food, excellent service, and wine with the dinner may cost about $5, including tip. Personal services such as haircuts, beauty parlor services, and the services of a household maid or cook are about half U.S. prices. Clothing is somewhat less expensive in Switzerland, and health services are much less costly.

Anyone who changes his legal residence to Switzerland no longer will pay U.S. city or State taxes. Taxes as residents of Switzerland are arranged locally on the basis of income estimated at roughly four or five times the rental of one's apartment. One will of course make arrangements with the aid of a tax accountant or an attorney at modest cost.

Typical Tax Haven

An incidental peek into a tax haven that has gained popularity recently, from the view of a corporation, or a man wishing to use a corporate structure, or related uses, can be seen from this account written by a journalist in Amsterdam about Curacao. This is basically from a bond issue aspect but it goes further and its implications in any case provide the flavor of tax havens in general, which fill an important corner in the international investment picture.

> Within the last few years, the Caribbean island of Curacao in the Netherlands Antilles has become the leading base for finance companies issuing Eurodollar bonds.
>
> Favorable tax rates and legal comforts are among the reasons.
>
> Laws governing corporations in Curacao are very flexible in comparison to those of Luxembourg, a main com-

petitor as a tax haven, according to Dutch bankers.

A Curacao concern can be set up with only one share-holder, and with capital in a foreign currency. In Luxembourg, the law is more complex, requiring more shareholders and more formalities, according to the Dutch.

Additionally there is investor concern that the pressure being brought on Luxembourg in recent years to align its policies more with those in other nations in the European Economic Community will lead to unfavorable conditions.

Tax on Interest Income

Net income of a Curacao finance company is subject to a corporate income tax at a rate of 2.4 percent on net income up to 100,000 guilders ($53,000) and 3 percent on net income over 100,000 guilders.

If the proceeds of a bond issue are lent to corporations in the United States, interest paid by the corporation to the Curacao finance company will qualify under the terms of the U.S.-Netherlands Antilles income tax convention, and be exempt from US withholding tax.

However, this interest income will be subject to Netherlands Antilles tax at a rate of 24 percent on net income up to 100,000 guilders and 30 percent on net income over 100,000 guilders.

In computing net income, the interest paid by the company on its outstanding bonds, which must be listed on a stock exchange, is deductible, provided that this net income—the difference between the interest received and interest paid—is at least 1 percent of the nominal amount of the outstanding bonds.

Thus if the finance company issues, say, $50 million nominal amount debentures, the net income must amount to at least $500,000 which will be taxed at a rate of 2.4 percent to 3 percent, where the proceeds of the bond issue are lent to a non-US corporation, and at a rate of 24 percent to 30 percent, where the proceeds are lent to a U.S. corporation.

Other features:

*Payments of interest by a Curacao company to holders of its bonds who are not residents of the Netherlands Antilles are not subject to Antilles income taxes, including withholding tax.

*The bonds are not subject to Netherlands Antilles inheritance taxes if held by persons not living there at the time of death.

Sources of Further Information

Investment in Japanese Stocks by Nomura Securities Ltd., price 360 yen, published by Institute of International Investment, 2 Kudan 3-chome, Chiyoda-ku, Tokyo, Japan. This is a concise handbook on all that the newcomer to Japanese securities should know about the mechanics of trading there.

Johannesburg Stock Exchange Monthly Bulletin, price 7.50 Rand per year plus R14.40 if you want it airmail. Obtainable from Public Relations Department, Johannesburg, Stock Exchange, P.O. Box 1174, Johannesburg, South Africa. Contains information of South African shares, including share capital, monthly volume, highs, lows, rights issues, etc.

Rand Daily Mail, P.O. Box 1138, Johannesburg, South Africa. South Africa daily newspaper giving daily statistics on South African stocks and general business and general news.

Financial Times, Bracken House, Cannon Street, London E.C.4, England. London's daily financial newspaper. Usually arrives in USA one day later. Probably the best financial newspaper in Europe or indeed in the world. Statistically covers stocks from not only London, but many parts of the world with an emphasis on places that are part of the Commonwealth. However, its financial news coverage is worldwide.

Le Monde, Paris. This daily French financial newspaper now puts out a condensed weekly English edition. Good coverage from the French point of view.

Neue Zuricher Zeitung, Zurich, Switzerland. The country's most authoritative newspaper. Publishes a world monthly review in English. For stock exchange information in Switzerland, see chapter on buying Swiss stocks.

Most central banks of the world put out a monthly bulletin on the economies of their respective countries and are available for the asking. Many US banks also occasionally publish information on investment opportunities abroad.

Stock exchanges of various countries can be written to, in care of the city and country, and they will either provide you with information, or else put you in touch with local financial information channels that communicate in English. Most big Swiss banks put out a brief monthly bulletin on stocks the world over.

Herald Tribune, Paris. This was originally a European sister to the New York newspaper of the same name but is now published in connection with the *New York Times* and the *Washington Post.* It is available throughout Europe in order that Americans as well as others interested in the US can follow the U.S. scene while abroad.

Financial Mail, P.O. Box 9959, Johannesburg, South Africa. A weekly newspaper of stock market news and prices.

South African Financial Gazette, P.O. Box 8161, Johannesburg, South Africa. A weekly publication devoted to news and views of the investment scene.

Mining Journal, 15 Wilson Street, London E.C.2, England. Probably the best publication anywhere on South African gold mines. Gives statistical data and comment. High quality. Monthly. Magazine size. $18.25 a year by air.

Kaffir Chart Service, published by Indicator Chart Service, Palisades Park, New Jersey 07650, USA. Weekly. Charts on leading South African gold shares, showing both London price and US ADR price.

International charts can be obtained individually from Investment Research, 36 Regent Street, Cambridge, England. They will provide a king-size chart of any foreign stock you ask for, if it is popularly traded and listed in the *Financial Times*. Not a chart service, but a good source for individual charts, especially English and Kaffirs and also leading European companies, some US & Canadian, etc.

Mines and Oils, a chart service of Canadian mining and oil companies. Weekly. Published by Fraser Research, 159 Bay Street, Toronto 1, Ontario, Canada. Single copy $6. Yearly: $55.

Offshore Funds

Earlier in this book we've dealt with offshore funds but perhaps without sufficient explanation in some areas. It's interesting to note that in early 1970 there were an unbelievable 193 international funds selling publicly to non-US residents. Most of them buy a sizable portion of US securities. While they generally deal only in stocks and bonds, a few invest in art, coins, stamps, ships, gold bullion, cattle, citrus groves, call options, and commodity futures. An example of one of these is the Midas Gold Fund, Panama registered, with headquarters sales office in Munich, Germany. Midas buys and sells gold bullion on the so-called free market (the market isn't really free if a majority of potential buyers are prohibited by their politicians from dealing in gold—as is the case with American citizens and British subjects).

Another of these unusual funds is the International Shipping Fund, Hamburg, which buys vessels or parts of vessels and hands them over to brokers for chartering. The IOS is the biggest and most famous of the offshore funds.

For those to whom the whole concept of offshore funds is a bit vague, let me insert here a newspaper columnist's reply to a reader who asks her London paper to explain them. While certain aspects are peculiar to the English scene, the general picture is widely applicable. The English of course are subject to strict exchange control. The column follows:

"Could you explain what an offshore fund is?" asks Mrs. E.M.S. of Wembley.

Basically an offshore fund is a unit trust established and managed overseas in order to benefit from various tax advantages. In the past two years or so numerous funds have been set up and several of the bigger unit trust management groups now operate this type of fund as well as their better known British trusts.

The fact that the funds are not allowed to advertise in Britain helps to explain the public's relative lack of knowledge about them. Advertising is prevented since they are not subject to the strict Board of Trade regulations covering unit trusts. For this reason management charges can be much higher than with a British unit trust.

Based in such havens as Bermuda, the Bahamas and the Channel Islands the funds are not only largely free of capital gains tax and income tax, but are able to adopt a more flexible worldwide investment policy.

The funds arrangements also largely avoid the inhibiting dollar premium costs on switching foreign investment.

This is one reason why the funds have attracted British purchasers in spite of the fact that they are liable to income tax and capital gains tax on selling the units (as well as the dollar premium).

Although gains would more likely be at long-term rates there is a danger that the Inland Revenue could assess British unitholders individually for their share of the fund's short-term gains. For those living outside this country, however, the tax advantages are obvious and some funds are only open to this sort of investor.

So far the records have been usually too short to judge performance of offshore funds although a falling Wall Street has not helped some in recent months.

Mirror, Mirror, on the Wall

This Gallup Poll may well influence your thinking on where your money is safest, or indeed where you yourself may be safest. In June 1970 Dr. George Gallup polled only the leading citizens of 40 nations. It was based on a scientifically selected sample of names from *The International Year Book* and the *Statesman's Who's Who*. They were asked: "What nation of the world do you think is best governed?"

The results may not be scientific or properly weighted for all financial factors, but they tend to be valid for our purposes. The winning nation must surely have merit. Here are the ratings in order:

1. Switzerland
2. Great Britain
3. Sweden
4. West Germany
5. Canada
6. United States
7. Denmark
8. Netherlands
9. Australia
10. Japan

With Switzerland in first place, I think the case this book has made is vindicated. A fitting note on which to end.

Index